Hollywood: A Very Short Introduction

VERY SHORT INTRODUCTIONS are for anyone wanting a stimulating and accessible way into a new subject. They are written by experts and have been translated into more than 40 different languages.

The series began in 1995 and now covers a wide variety of topics in every discipline. The VSI library now contains more than 400 volumes—a Very Short Introduction to everything from Indian philosophy to psychology and American history—and continues to grow in every subject area.

Very Short Introductions available now:

ACCOUNTING Christopher Nobes
ADVERTISING Winston Fletcher
AFRICAN AMERICAN RELIGION
  Eddie S. Glaude Jr
AFRICAN HISTORY John Parker
  and Richard Rathbone
AFRICAN RELIGIONS
  Jacob K. Olupona
AGNOSTICISM Robin Le Poidevin
ALEXANDER THE GREAT
  Hugh Bowden
ALGEBRA Peter M. Higgins
AMERICAN HISTORY Paul S. Boyer
AMERICAN IMMIGRATION
  David A. Gerber
AMERICAN LEGAL HISTORY
  G. Edward White
AMERICAN POLITICAL
  HISTORY Donald Critchlow
AMERICAN POLITICAL PARTIES
  AND ELECTIONS L. Sandy Maisel
AMERICAN POLITICS
  Richard M. Valelly
THE AMERICAN PRESIDENCY
  Charles O. Jones
THE AMERICAN REVOLUTION
  Robert J. Allison
AMERICAN SLAVERY
  Heather Andrea Williams
THE AMERICAN WEST Stephen Aron
AMERICAN WOMEN'S
  HISTORY Susan Ware
ANAESTHESIA Aidan O'Donnell
ANARCHISM Colin Ward
ANCIENT ASSYRIA Karen Radner
ANCIENT EGYPT Ian Shaw

ANCIENT EGYPTIAN ART AND
  ARCHITECTURE Christina Riggs
ANCIENT GREECE Paul Cartledge
THE ANCIENT NEAR EAST
  Amanda H. Podany
ANCIENT PHILOSOPHY Julia Annas
ANCIENT WARFARE
  Harry Sidebottom
ANGELS David Albert Jones
ANGLICANISM Mark Chapman
THE ANGLO-SAXON AGE John Blair
THE ANIMAL KINGDOM
  Peter Holland
ANIMAL RIGHTS David DeGrazia
THE ANTARCTIC Klaus Dodds
ANTISEMITISM Steven Beller
ANXIETY Daniel Freeman and
  Jason Freeman
THE APOCRYPHAL GOSPELS
  Paul Foster
ARCHAEOLOGY Paul Bahn
ARCHITECTURE Andrew Ballantyne
ARISTOCRACY William Doyle
ARISTOTLE Jonathan Barnes
ART HISTORY Dana Arnold
ART THEORY Cynthia Freeland
ASTROBIOLOGY David C. Catling
ATHEISM Julian Baggini
AUGUSTINE Henry Chadwick
AUSTRALIA Kenneth Morgan
AUTISM Uta Frith
THE AVANT GARDE David Cottington
THE AZTECS David Carrasco
BACTERIA Sebastian G. B. Amyes
BARTHES Jonathan Culler
THE BEATS David Sterritt

Available soon:

MEDIEVAL PHILOSOPHY
    John Marenbon
SLANG Jonathon Green

EARTH SYSTEM SCIENCE Tim Lenton
THE WELFARE STATE David Garland
CRYSTALLOGRAPHY A. M. Glazer

For more information visit our web site

www.oup.com/vsi/

Peter Decherney

HOLLYWOOD

A Very Short Introduction

OXFORD
UNIVERSITY PRESS

Oxford University Press is a department of the
University of Oxford. It furthers the University's objective
of excellence in research, scholarship, and education
by publishing worldwide.

Oxford   New York

Auckland   Cape Town   Dar es Salaam   Hong Kong   Karachi
Kuala Lumpur   Madrid   Melbourne   Mexico City   Nairobi
New Delhi   Shanghai   Taipei   Toronto

With offices in

Argentina   Austria   Brazil   Chile   Czech Republic   France   Greece
Guatemala   Hungary   Italy   Japan   Poland   Portugal   Singapore
South Korea   Switzerland   Thailand   Turkey   Ukraine   Vietnam

Oxford is a registered trade mark of Oxford University Press
in the UK and certain other countries.

Published in the United States of America by
Oxford University Press
198 Madison Avenue, New York, NY 10016

Library of Congress Cataloging-in-Publication Data
Decherney, Peter.
Hollywood : a very short introduction / Peter Decherney.
Pages   cm. — (Very short introductions)
Includes bibliographical references and index.
ISBN 978-0-19-994354-8 (paperback)
1. Motion picture industry—California—Los Angeles—History.
2. Motion pictures—California—Los Angeles—History.   I. Title.
PN1993.5.U65D44   2015
384'.80979494—dc23   2015015111

Printed by Integrated Books International, United States of America
on acid-free paper

for Sophia and Asher

Contents

List of illustrations

Acknowledgments

"I have made this [letter] longer than usual because I have not had time to make it shorter," Blaise Pascal once wrote. If I have been successful in condensing a century of Hollywood's history into this short book, it is because I have enjoyed a decade of discussing the subject with students at the University of Pennsylvania. Their insightful questions and looks of recognition or confusion have helped me hone the story, identify trends, and fill in the necessary backstory. This book has also benefited from generous careful readings by John Belton, Julie Corman, Dana Polan, Emily Steiner, Robert Steiner, my editor Nancy Toff, and an anonymous reader for Oxford University Press. The book is dedicated to my children, Sophia and Asher, who have both seen many more black and white films than their years would suggest.

Introduction: Five theses on the history of Hollywood

This is a short history of Hollywood from the pre-Hollywood days of Thomas Edison to the world of ubiquitous online video. It discusses many films and filmmakers, but the main focus is on the big picture: the adoption of new technologies, responses to competition from independent filmmakers, and the impact of the political and cultural tumult of Hollywood's first century. One advantage of a short history is that readers can get an overview before delving more deeply into specific periods or questions. Another advantage is that compressing the history allows us to see patterns that might be lost in a longer work.

Trying to give a complete and up-to-the-minute history, I have synthesized the latest academic research and theories about Hollywood into what I hope is a readable text. I have also drawn on my own books, class lectures, and thinking about film and media history. So even readers who are familiar with the names, films, and events of Hollywood's history should find much that is new in this book. I begin with five briefly stated observations about how and why Hollywood has developed before launching into the history.

1. Nothing natural

Why did 35mm become the standard width of Hollywood film? Why are feature films usually 90–120 minutes long? Why are movie stars used to sell films and television shows? The earliest histories of Hollywood relayed stories of pioneers uncovering essential filmmaking techniques through experimentation and discovery. But there is nothing natural or inevitable about the way moving images are used to tell stories. No individual or group of people discovered filmmaking. Historical, cultural, economic, and political forces all came together to shape the art and industry of Hollywood.

2. Risky business

Making movies is an inherently risky business. Once Procter & Gamble developed Pringles potato chips, the company could keep stamping them out forever. But film is neither a commodity nor a stable enterprise. Research and development rarely pay off, and the success of one film does not ensure the success of the next one. Much of the design of Hollywood's studio system can be explained as strategies for managing the risks entailed in creating expensive, collaborative, and unique products. Hollywood's reliance on movie stars and genre films are only the most obvious attempts to build some predictability into moviemaking and the moviegoing experience. Most elements of the studio system have been developed to minimize risk and ensure predictability, including the creation of an organization to police the morality of films, the concentration of ownership through mergers and acquisitions, the cultivation of media franchises, and the leveraging of audience data.

3. "Hollyworld"

Hollywood has always been a global business based in Los Angeles. After World War I, Hollywood established a worldwide distribution network that has only grown more complete during the past century. And other countries' attempts to place limits on the circulation of Hollywood films through quotas or financial regulation have rarely been effective. From very early on, Hollywood made films to appeal to a global audience, and its talent magnet has consistently brought the world's best actors, directors, and writers to Los Angeles. Since the 1910s, the US government has devoted significant resources to helping Hollywood succeed as a global industry, and Hollywood is sometimes seen as a mechanism for Americanizing the world. But the studio system has always been both a receptacle for and a disseminator of global culture, equally Hollywoodizing America and the rest of the world.

4. Transmedia

Movies have also always been one medium in a chain of "transmedia" storytelling and consumption. The earliest films were adapted from news stories, cartoons, and popular theater. They were shown in vaudeville houses and at fairgrounds, and they were used to sell cigarettes, clothing, and other merchandise. To take one perfect example, when Walt Disney's *Snow White and the Seven Dwarfs* (1937) premiered, the company had merchandising agreements with more than seventy different companies, including makers of dinnerware, toys, and storybooks. In the 1960s, studios became part of multimedia conglomerates intent on producing what have come to be called "tent-pole franchises:" stories and characters that unfold across all of a company's divisions. The internet has drawn media consumers into the transmedia process as well, and fans create and share their own remixes and mashups as an essential part of the Hollywood ecosystem. Warner Bros. profits come from advertising placed next to feminist retellings of the *Harry Potter* series as well as from theater ticket sales and television licensing.

5. The more things change

Hollywood is in a state of constant change and perpetual crisis. There is always a new technology, an independent film movement, or a global financial crisis on the horizon. And yet for over a century the studio system has not only remained intact; it has grown more powerful and pervasive. To be sure, some studios have gone under and others are relatively young, but since the 1910s eight or so companies have controlled the vast majority of the media consumed around the world. Competition from independent companies, new media platforms, and even piracy have been a constant part of Hollywood's history, always challenging the system to change and grow. And despite the alarmist rhetoric that has been a staple of Hollywood culture, the studio system has long been and is likely to remain at the top of the global media economy.

Chapter 1
Before Hollywood

New media always grow out of existing media, and film is no exception. Both early film technology and storytelling methods developed from older media. Most early film projectors, for example, were simply magic lantern slide projectors with jury-rigged film reels bolted on. The new technology (film) was grafted onto the older technology (slides). The aesthetic and narrative styles of early films were similarly lifted from newspaper comics, photography, vaudeville, and magic lantern shows. Film was never a new medium but always an outgrowth and mixture of many others.

From the phonograph to the Vitascope

Indeed, when inventor Thomas Edison set his company to work designing a film camera, he wrote that his goal was to do "for the eye what the phonograph does for the ear." Edison had already developed a successful phonograph business, and he wanted to replicate it with moving pictures, adapting the phonograph experience and commercial model to the visual realm. The phonograph division of the Edison Manufacturing Company specialized in installing phonographs in storefront parlors, where patrons could move from one machine to the next, listening to popular songs or speeches recorded on Edison's own record label.

Following that model, Edison's company developed peep-show viewers called Kinetoscopes, which displayed a minute or so of film to a patron who looked through the viewfinder. Popular subjects included boxing matches and passion plays, which could be broken down into scenes that unfolded as viewers moved from one Kinetoscope to the next, depositing coins at each turn. Other Kinetoscope films took advantage of the peep-show design, showing scenes that looked as if they had been filmed through a

1. Boxing films were popular on Edison's peep-show viewer, the Kinetoscope, before he abandoned it in favor of movie projection. Some critics have argued that mobile phones bring us back to the Kinetoscope's individual viewing experience.

keyhole. Edison never lost sight of his goal: joining image and sound. He eventually filed a patent for a Kinetophone to display synchronized images and sounds, although only a few were made, and they never worked very well.

Edison was far from the only inventor working to develop motion picture technology. A number of inventors in the United States and Europe simultaneously devised similar machines, often learning from each other. Unlike Edison, however, most of his rivals had dreams of projecting moving images onto large screens, not showing them to individuals peering through small holes. (Later commenters have mused that watching movies on portable devices like mobile phones takes us full circle, back to Edison's original peep-show model.)

When a projector designed by two French photographic equipment company owners, the Lumière brothers, began to be used in vaudeville houses in New York in 1896, it quickly became clear that projected images were a hit with audiences. Edison realized that he needed to rethink the direction of his film business. Rather than return to the laboratory, Edison bought the rights to a projector designed by two recent engineering school graduates, Thomas Armat and Charles Frances Jenkins, marketing the device as "Edison's Vitascope," with a small plaque crediting the original designers.

As he had with the phonograph, Edison went into the film production business to create content for his machines. He built a small film studio, known as the Black Maria, on the grounds of his West Orange, New Jersey, laboratory. Black Maria was slang for the police trucks used to transport prisoners, and it suggested the unseemly subjects being filmed—or at least that was how they were perceived. Many of the Edison Company's earliest films were of vaudeville performers, who came up from New York to have their routines recorded for the Wizard of Menlo Park, as Edison was known. A succession of strong men, dancers, and animal acts performed within the black, tar-covered walls of Edison's studio. The only light source was the sun, which shone in through the retractable roof. The entire building spun around 360 degrees to catch the light all day long. Other filmmakers built glass studios to let in the sunlight, and many films were shot outside in the direct sunlight. It would be another decade before lights were strong enough and film stock sensitive enough to allow artificial light to be used to illuminate filmed subjects. Using available light, early camera operators captured exotic vistas, newsworthy events, and scenes of everyday life, all called "actualities."

As early as 1894 (and possibly 1893), Edison began depositing his films at the Library of Congress so that they would receive copyright protection. The company printed its films on long strips of paper—known as paper prints—and registered them as photographs with the Copyright Office of the Library of Congress. Because paper prints of so many Edison films were deposited in a government vault, they continue to exist, even though more than 90 percent of films made before 1910 have vanished.

2. Edison's studio, the Black Maria, could spin 360 degrees to let sunlight in all day long. It was not until around 1913 that more sensitive film stock and more powerful bulbs made it possible to shoot movies using only artificial light.

The nickelodeon era

The earliest films were shown at amusement parks, vaudeville houses, and curiosity displays called dime museums. The first dedicated movie theaters, nickelodeons, began to appear around 1903. Nickelodeons were generally storefronts that had been fitted with a projector and a screen. Often they were converted saloons, and the transition from saloon to nickelodeon is significant. Saloons were spaces for working-class men to spend newly won leisure time and money. The conversion of saloons to nickelodeons indicated that working-class women and children were entering the space of public leisure entertainment. A family could stop in to a nickelodeon while shopping, stay for an hour or two, and then leave. The show of short films, however, went on all day, much like television programming would later. The mixing of genders, ages, classes, and ethnic communities in the space of the theater deterred many potential middle-class customers at first. Legislators soon took action. In New York, one provision stipulated that the lights in a nickelodeon had to be bright enough for a patron to read the newspaper, suggesting that nickelodeons might be places for middle-class leisure pursuits like reading the paper and not just a haven for pickpockets, "mashers" (sexual predators), and customers there to consume prurient images.

Although nickelodeons were potentially new democratic spaces, they were also deeply local. Films were short and could be shown in many different combinations. Musical accompaniment varied widely; one nickelodeon might have a piano player and another a jazz band playing alongside the same films. Some had actors who voiced characters and most had narrators to introduce and explain films. Whatever the setup, silent films were rarely shown silently. Many nickelodeons also had only one projector, so live entertainment or lantern slides were still used during reel changes. Nickelodeons were multimedia experiences, and viewing a movie was very different if you watched it on Manhattan's Lower East Side, in nearby Chinatown, or halfway across the country in

Chicago's Loop. Films were mass-produced, but film viewing was far from a homogenous experience.

The short films projected in nickelodeons could be mixed and matched to produce very different experiences, and the exhibitor—the person arranging the show—was often the most creative individual behind the program. In some cases, exhibitors went on to become directors, most notably Edwin S. Porter, who rose from dime museum exhibitor to Edison's top director (*The Great Train Robbery*, 1903). Nickelodeons were also an easy way to enter the emerging industry, and many Hollywood moguls began as nickelodeon owners, including Carl Laemmle (who founded Universal), Adolph Zukor (who cofounded Paramount), and Louis B. Mayer (who cofounded MGM).

Pre-1908 films have come to be known as "the cinema of attractions," because they emphasized spectacle, motion, and shock. Filmmakers placed cameras on trains, boats, and amusement park rides to capture the pace of modern life. They filmed world leaders and famous monuments. They offered virtual travel and vicarious thrills. Edison's 1896 film *The May Irwin–John Rice Kiss*, to take a popular example, remained on screens for years, and it was often repeated several times for the same audience. The film showed two portly actors engaging in a chaste kiss in a scene from a popular play, and it perfectly represented the power of film. As viewers of the film, we have a privileged close-up of the actors, a better view than even the best seat in the theater could offer. Moreover, the story is removed, offering only the most talked-about spectacle, or attraction, of the production: the kiss.

Other films played with the idea of the invisible fourth wall, separating the audience from the film. They showed salacious or dangerous scenes and then reminded the audience of their protected, voyeuristic position. A 1901 British film, *The Big Swallow*, for example, showed a close-up of a man walking toward the camera. Eventually the camera seems to descend down the man's throat, and the screen turns black. Then we see a pair of legs fall into the cavernous black space. At first it appears as though the man has swallowed us—the audience—calling attention to the safe space of the theater in which no image could, in reality, physically harm us. But then we realize that the man in the film has seemingly swallowed the cameraman, and we are reminded of another displacement; we are reminded that the film is not live and was in fact filmed by an unseen technology, a camera, and by an offscreen cinematographer. Films like *The Big Swallow* trained early film audiences to experience the new virtuality of film and the voyeuristic experience of spectatorship.

Despite the common myth that it took years before filmmakers started telling stories, narrative films were prevalent from the earliest days of cinema. The stories were often based on existing material. Films recreated newspaper comics or old vaudeville routines. Many films required audiences to be familiar with the stories that the films illustrated, what film scholars often call "intertexts." Early film audiences had narrators to explain the action, but it helped if you already knew the biblical story of Judith and Holofernes, for example, or *King Lear*, or the plots of Broadway plays. *Uncle Tom's Cabin*, for example, was the most popular American play of the nineteenth century and still a popular attraction in the early 1900s. Many companies, including Edison's, made screen versions, staging highlights from the play for the film audience. If the audience did not know the intertexts—the novel and the play—they would be lost, although one could of course enjoy the sheer spectacle of the scenes.

Around 1908–1909, filmmaking and the film industry underwent a number of changes. Established film companies started to court a middle-class audience in order to expand the industry's reach. Production companies made films based on novels and Broadway plays. And stories began to be told in new ways. In particular, filmmakers took over the job of narration from the live narrators in the theaters. Edison's version of *Uncle Tom's Cabin* (1903) is a perfect example of a film made before this transformation. It is presented as a series of scenes with a cut—an edit—between each one. It is as if the curtain dropped and rose again between each shot. The filmmakers left it to the audience and the nickelodeon narrators to fill in the gaps.

Films made during the 1908–1909 change began to use a codified system of "continuity editing" to visually give the audience the most important pieces of information. Filmmakers developed a stylistic system to let audiences understand how two shots are connected in space and time while also relating characters' thoughts and feelings.

When a character looks offscreen in one direction and we see a vista through a window in the next shot, we know that we are approximating the character's gaze. This is called an "eyeline match." Similarly, when a character begins to exit through a door in one shot and we pick up the same character completing the action in the next shot, we know the two shots are connected. It is a "match on action." This stylistic code often seems natural and obvious to us, but it is in fact a human innovation, influenced by culture, technology, and history. It is the most basic but also one of the most amazing elements of film: spectators are able to construct a coherent idea of story time and space from the short fragments of film spliced together.

Other elements that helped filmmakers narrate their stories around the same time include intertitles, the cards of description or dialogue that were shown between shots. Intertitles directly usurped the job of live narrators, and they looked forward to dialogue in sound film.

Acting too saw a transformation. The exaggerated pantomime that we associate with early film became less popular during this period, and a more contained realistic style began to dominate.

The broad gestures early film actors used to express emotions, as they had in the nineteenth-century theater, were replaced by subtle facial expressions glimpsed in close-up. Hungarian film theorist Béla Balázs called these close-ups "silent soliloquies." Filmmakers had been experimenting with editing and different acting styles from early on, but this new unified style of storytelling took over very quickly.

One 1907 film, Edwin S. Porter's *The Teddy Bears*, shows the industry right on the cusp of these changes. It combines two stories: the fairy tale "Goldilocks and the Three Bears" and the then-recent news story of President Teddy Roosevelt's hunting expedition. Roosevelt started a national craze for stuffed "teddy" bears when, on a hunting trip, he spared a baby cub after orphaning it. Such was the state of early twentieth-century animal rights. In the film, Goldilocks sits in the bears' chairs, eats their porridge, and is sleeping in the baby bear's bed when the bear family returns. Goldilocks flees and is chased by the bears, only to run into President Roosevelt. Roosevelt, the hero of the story, shoots the mother and father bear, shackles the baby as a present for Goldilocks, and, in addition, gives Goldilocks a collection of stuffed teddy bears she had admired in the house.

Scholars have puzzled over the film's meaning for decades. But one thing is clear; it combines the elements of the pre- and post-1908 cinematic storytelling. Like the early nickelodeon films, it requires knowledge of other stories. It even contains a keyhole film within it: Goldilocks spies on the stuffed teddy bears through the keyhole of a wooden door while they do acrobatic stunts in a still-impressive animated stop-motion sequence. But the film also looks forward: the acting alternates between the histrionic pantomime of early cinema and the realistic mode of later films. The editing style also reveals the film to be stuck between two aesthetic paradigms. In the opening sequence of the film each shot is a separate scene, but the final chase sequence relies on the direction of the action to connect shots within a scene. Although the moral of *The Teddy Bears* feels foreign to us today, the visual storytelling method is more familiar than many of its antecedents.

The Trust and the independents

In addition to undergoing a major change in storytelling methods between 1907 and 1909, the American film industry was also restructured. The first film companies in the United States engaged in fierce competition. The larger companies hired away talent from their competitors. Producers "duped" (copied) each other's films and sold them as their own. The leaders of the industry also attempted to monopolize the market by asserting sweeping intellectual property claims. Edison, in particular, aggressively pursued litigation in an attempt to wipe out the competition, and, for a brief period, his tactics proved successful.

Edison held three broad patents on motion picture technology, and in court cases and the trade press he regularly claimed that all moviemaking endeavors were built on his inventions. Eventually, Edison's patent claims were all overturned in court, although he reapplied and managed to claim credit for a few minor adjustments. But court losses did not stop Edison or his company from dragging other companies through legal battles that they could not afford to fight. It reveals a lot about the centrality of litigation to Edison's business that the head of his legal department, Frank Dyer, rose to be the head of Edison's entire film division.

Edison's most formidable competitor was a company called American Mutoscope and Biograph, or Biograph for short. Biograph's camera and projector had been designed in part by Edison's former chief of motion picture development, W. K. L. Dickson, and the company claimed that its equipment was significantly different from Edison's. More importantly, Biograph held the exclusive rights to one of the key film patents: the Latham loop. Patented by chemistry professor Woodville

Latham, the Latham loop simply involves leaving a bit of slack in the filmstrip before and after it enters the gate of the projector, where light shines through it. One reason that early films were so short is that tension would build up in the projector, and the celluloid would break. The Latham loop absorbed the tension and allowed filmmakers to make longer films. No exhibitor could show a film without using the Latham loop, and it became one of the key pieces of intellectual property in the early American film industry.

In December 1908, Edison and Biograph agreed to pool their patents and set up the Motion Picture Patents Company (the Trust), a group of companies that also included celluloid manufacturer George Eastman and a number of US and European film producers and distributors. The Trust agreement was a Faustian pact for distributors and exhibitors. They gained access to the Trust's exclusive technology and films, but they lost their autonomy and were forced to pay licensing fees that made it hard to turn a profit.

The Trust sought to standardize the industry, making film into a commodity rather than a unique good. No two films have exactly the same audience appeal, but the Trust treated all films equally. Producers had to meet a quota, and films were released on a set day of the week. Films were sold in reels, and every reel was sold at the same price, like pounds of sugar. Distributors also had to buy films in advance, sight unseen.

In its efforts to standardize the industry, the Trust even embraced censorship. Starting in 1909, the Trust agreed to let the National Board of Censorship, later renamed the National Board of Review, stamp each film with its seal of approval. As part of the effort to attract middle-class patrons and deter politicians eager to win votes by imposing restrictions on movie theaters, exhibitors wanted to make themselves appear more respectable. They agreed to show only films that had been approved by the National Board of Review. And once the Board had an exclusive agreement with the Trust, even more exhibitors became exclusive Trust licensees.

The Trust held a tight grip on every aspect of the industry, from the sale of film stock to the approval of the censor board. But standardization deterred innovation and bred dissention. The independents who opposed the Trust incorporated as Independent Moving Pictures (IMP) only ten days after the Trust itself. Led by film distributor Carl Laemmle, the independents bought film stock from the Lumière brothers' company in France, and they established their own network outside of the Trust's. The Trust had fixed its business methods just as the industry was in the process of changing, and it could not keep up with audience demands. The independents, on the other hand, exploited innovations that brought in the middle-class audiences so important to the next phase of industry growth.

First, the independents started to make feature films. Where the Trust insisted on selling films by the reel (about fifteen minutes each), the independents' longer multireel films were better suited to the adaptations of plays and novels that appealed to middle-class patrons. The independents also imported spectacular Italian epics, which enjoyed a vogue in the United States at the time. The Trust members did release some films with stories that stretched across multiple reels, but in general they missed the opportunity to move into feature film production.

Second, the independents realized the value of movie stars. Movies come and go, but the actors continually reappear. Edison's first instinct had been to bring vaudeville stars to his studio and capture their performances on film. But many Trust members resisted the idea of promoting movie stars or even crediting the actors in films. They knew that once actors had marquee value, they would demand higher salaries. Audiences, however, clamored to know more about the faces they saw every week.

Reporters began to refer to Biograph's popular actress Florence Lawrence as the Biograph Girl long before audiences knew her name. Carl Laemmle hired Lawrence for IMP in 1909, and he promoted her as a movie star, circulating sensational stories about her private life and forthcoming films. Other independent producers capitalized on the demand for stars by luring stage talent to the screen. Nickelodeon owner Adolph Zukor based his production company on the rise of star appeal, calling it the Famous Players Film Company and importing a French film about Queen Elizabeth I starring the legendary actress Sarah Bernhardt.

As quickly as the Trust gained control of the industry, it lost its grip. It is as if the Hollywood studios were replaced by internet video companies in the space of only a few years. In addition to being left behind in the move to feature films and the star system, the Trust experienced a number of legal and operational blows. In 1911, the Eastman Company's agreement with the Trust ended, and it began to supply film stock to the independents. Then the Latham Loop patent expired, and Trust member Kalem lost a landmark copyright case.

Backed by the legal resources of the Trust, Kalem defended its right to adapt books and plays without permission or payment. Most film companies before the Kalem decision specialized in unauthorized adaptations. It was not clear whether filmmakers needed permission to create filmed versions of popular works of literature, and they created adaptations of the bestselling novels and Broadway shows at will.

The case reached the Supreme Court, where the justices decided that film producers do in fact need permission to adapt works from other media. The resolution of the case initiated a race for film companies to strike exclusive arrangements with publishers and producers. The Trust members were outmaneuvered by the independents, who grabbed up the best partnerships, and by 1913 the Trust had been all but supplanted by the independents. In 1916 the Trust was found to be in violation of the Sherman Antitrust Act of 1890 and broken up. This was the final nail in the coffin for an organization that quickly went from total control of the US film industry to being a calcified relic unable to meet market demands.

Chapter 2
The studio system

Carl Laemmle, Adolph Zukor, William Fox, and the other
independents overthrew the Trust, only to form their own closely
linked group of industry power brokers—what economists call an
oligopoly. The independents moved to California and founded the
Hollywood studios, including Universal, Paramount, and Fox.
Ever since, Hollywood has been dominated by eight or so
companies, although the ranks of major studios have been
shuffled many times. Much like the Trust, the Hollywood studios
set out to standardize the industry through corporate control and
risk management strategies. But Hollywood has proven to be
more resilient than Edison and his partners.

The birth of the studios

Even before the Trust fell apart, the independents relocated
film production from New York and New Jersey to Los Angeles.
The story that the independents moved west to escape Edison's
clutches is often repeated, but the real reasons were much more
practical (and Trust members were actually some of the first
studios to reach the West Coast). Most movies were still shot
using sunlight. Studios searched for longer winter days in
Florida, Mexico, and even Cuba, but Los Angeles proved to be
the best option. In Los Angeles, producers enjoyed good weather
all year long, and within a few hours they could reach a wide

variety of locations, traveling to the desert, beach, mountains, and farm country of southern California. Los Angeles was also a non-union town, and the studios could avoid the expenses of organized labor, at least until film technicians unionized under the Studio Basic Agreement of 1921. All of the studios continued to maintain finance offices in New York, which they consulted daily, and some film production continued on the East Coast, too, largely to take advantage of Broadway talent. But by 1922, 84 percent of American film production was based in the Los Angeles area.

A number of mergers in the 1910s led to the consolidation of the Hollywood studios. As they became vertically integrated, combining every aspect of filmmaking and delivery, production companies joined with distributors and theater chains as well. Distributor W. W. Hodkinson, for example, merged several statewide distributors to form the first national chain specializing in feature films, the Paramount Pictures Corporation.

Paramount attracted top feature film producers Adolph Zukor and Jesse Lasky, who had recently hired a new director named Cecil B. DeMille. Eventually, Paramount merged with its producers and theater owners (known as exhibitors), and together they became a powerful entity able to bully the exhibitors who were not already in its network. Exhibitors relied on Paramount's stable of stars and exclusive adaptation deals with Broadway companies, and Paramount insisted that theater owners rent the studio's entire season of films or nothing, a practice known as "block booking." Since the theater owners needed to commit to the films even before many of them had been shot, they were booked "blind," sight unseen, as well. The Supreme Court eventually banned the practice of block booking as anticompetitive, but not until after World War II.

Big budget "A" movies would premiere at the top movie palaces like the Strand Theater in Times Square, where they were accompanied by live performances, orchestras, and often product giveaways. After a period of time, the films moved on to the lower rung of theaters, where they were shown with less fanfare but at a cheaper price. In the industry parlance of the time, the films "cleared" their "zones," and it could take up to two years for a film to make its way through all of the zones before finally ending its run at a rural movie house. In fact, one large collection of previously lost films was discovered buried under an ice skating rink in Canada, where they had been deposited and unwittingly preserved in the cold ground after completing their long run through the North American theater circuit.

The studios' reach extended far beyond the United States, and after World War I Hollywood became the global industry leader that it remains. Before the war, France had dominated the world's film market, with Italy a distant second. European film companies, however, were forced to reduce their operations during the war, turning over personnel and facilities to the war effort and leaving theaters with little to show after the armistice.

As the European film industries rebuilt, Hollywood studios filled the vacuum. They set up international distribution subsidiaries and flooded screens in Europe and throughout the world with American films. When one of Hollywood's biggest rivals in the 1920s, the German studio Ufa, ran into financial trouble, Paramount and MGM bailed it out with a $4 million loan that ensured the two Hollywood studios would get distribution priority in Germany. They called the new venture Parufamet.

To expedite international distribution, many Hollywood films were shot with two cameras in order to produce dual negatives. Once the negatives were cut, one set would remain in Los Angeles to strike prints for domestic distribution, and the second would be sent to London, the hub of international distribution. Hollywood's international revenues continued to rise, and by 1953 international sales surpassed domestic box office profits.

Hollywood's global dominance caused a crisis in Europe, where a number of countries sought to protect their markets from American saturation. Germany, England, and other countries imposed quotas on the importation of Hollywood films, and eventually European countries banded together to attempt to rival America. Under the auspices of the League of Nations, the Film Europe movement promoted European cinema while blocking Hollywood. The United States responded by setting up a State Department film office to negotiate better trade agreements for Hollywood. The US Congress also passed the Webb-Pomerene Act (1918), allowing Hollywood and other industries to work together overseas in ways that would have constituted illegal collusion in the United States.

In 1922 the studios started their own organization, the Motion Picture Producers and Distributors of America (MPPDA), run by former postmaster general Will Hays. Hays and the MPPDA later became known as Hollywood's censors, but in the early 1920s, working from his New York office, Hays lobbied Congress on Hollywood's behalf, while the MPPDA's international division pushed for smoother global distribution.

Hays also worked to redefine Hollywood's image, highlighting the central role of films in spreading American culture and products globally. "Every foot of American film," Hays often repeated, "sells $1.00 worth of manufactured products some place in the world." In other speeches, Hays claimed, "The motion picture carries to every American at home, and to millions of purchasers abroad, the visual, vivid perception of American manufactured products."

Ironically, what became the classical Hollywood style of filmmaking had been an international style before World War I. Films circulated rapidly, and filmmakers learned from each other in a global conversation about film art. But once Hollywood dominated world film distribution, European countries began to develop new national styles to distinguish their films in the market. There are many cultural, political, and aesthetic reasons for the emergence of

German Expressionist film, French Impressionist film, and other national styles in the 1920s. But one motivation clearly was finding a way to stand apart from and compete with Hollywood.

Back in Los Angeles, the new moguls restructured the studios, rationalizing filmmaking and turning it into an art that could be practiced on an industrial scale. Many of the changes to film production methods were pioneered by the precocious producer Thomas Ince. Ince made some of the most important films of the 1910s, including *The Italian* (1915) and *Civilization* (1916). He also owned a large studio, Inceville, for several years, before embarking on a series of partnerships with other moguls. Ince did all of this before he died at the age of forty-two, just a few days after celebrating his birthday on William Randolph Hearst's yacht. Ince officially died of heart failure, but the legend that he died from bullet wounds inflicted by Hearst continues to stimulate the imaginations of historians, novelists, and filmmakers.

Before Inceville, film studios tended to have autonomous teams of collaborators who came up with ideas and brought them to fruition, like individual chemistry laboratories working independently under the same roof to share overhead costs. This was how D. W. Griffith worked at Biograph, where his close-knit production unit included cameraman Billy Bitzer and actresses Lillian and Dorothy Gish.

Inceville, on the other hand, was a top-down and efficient system. Ince simultaneously oversaw five shooting stages. Every film was preceded by a "continuity script" that laid it out shot by shot. With a detailed blueprint, every aspect of production could be managed more systematically. Scenes could be filmed out of sequence, and actors and other personnel only had to appear on sets when they were needed. Film crews became highly specialized, so there was an economical division of labor. Soon, all of the studios became moviemaking factories—dream factories, as they were sometimes called.

Although the moguls who built the studios were all men, in its early days, Hollywood had many women working on both the creative and business sides of the industry. Some of Hollywood's most prolific and successful screenwriters were women, including

3. Film pioneer Alice Guy-Blaché directed more than one thousand films and was one of the first women to manage her own studio.

Anita Loos, Louis Weber, and two-time Academy Award–winner Frances Marion. Weber also had a successful directing career, and Alice Guy-Blaché, who owned her own production company, is said to have directed over one thousand films stretching from 1890s French shorts to 1920s American features. Screenwriter June Mathis became one of the most powerful executives in the industry, holding high-level positions at Metro and Goldwyn Pictures (both would later become part of MGM) and Famous Players–Lasky (which became part of Paramount). By the 1930s, however, many fewer women could be found behind the camera. Dorothy Arzner was the most successful and one of the few women who directed studio films during the 1930s and 1940s, and Arzner's distinctive voice was important. She created strong female roles for many top stars, including Lucille Ball, Clara Bow, Katharine Hepburn, and Rosalind Russell.

The star system

The studios also brought more stability to their business through branding and consistent storytelling. Over time, each studio developed its own distinct house style. MGM celebrated the glamour of its stars. "More stars than there are in heaven," the studio's publicity department boasted. Paramount was known for its European sex symbols like Marlene Dietrich, while Warner Bros. specialized in grittier films geared towards an urban working-class audience. Since many of the studios owned theater chains and dealt regularly with the same exhibitors, they also had detailed demographic information about their ticket buyers.

Nevertheless, every studio diversified its offerings in order to reach a range of theatergoers and weather changes in taste. In addition to its gangster films, for example, Warner Bros. adapted literary fare for John Barrymore. And Warner Bros. discovered a new market for musicals with Busby Berkeley's depression-era hits like *42nd Street*, *Gold Diggers of 1933*, and *Footlight Parade* (all 1933). Most studios also made a few prestige pictures every year, calculated to improve the studio's reputation even if the films did not turn a profit. At the first Oscar ceremony in 1929, the Academy of Motion Picture Arts and Sciences recognized both the commercial and artistic sides of studio output, giving top awards to both the best picture of the year and the most "unique and artistic" picture.

The studios' most stable commodities were their stars. Stars had always had a place in the American movie business. Edison's first films, we have already seen, featured vaudeville stars in the hope of bringing established audiences to the new medium. Later, the independents capitalized on well-known theater stars in their bid to draw middle-class patrons to the movies.

Stars promise repetition and consistency, counteracting the uncertainties of filmmaking. Over time, the studios developed a system for crafting and controlling star personas that would remain stable across films and keep moviegoers' attention with publicity between new releases. The English-born Charles Chaplin played a series of different roles before discovering the Little Tramp character that he would play into the sound era. The Little Tramp wore the same hat, pants, and shoes from film to film, and he always exuded pathos and resilience as he failed at work but (often) triumphed in love.

Chaplin's devotion to a single character was extreme, but it was only an amplification of the consistency offered by other stars. Humphrey Bogart played Bogie whether he was a club owner in North Africa or a Los Angeles private detective. Katharine Hepburn played Katharine Hepburn whether she was a Philadelphia socialite or a New York reporter.

It almost always took time to refine a star's image. In his first films, for example, Cary Grant (born Archibald Leach in Bristol, England) did not play the suave, comic, well-dressed leading man that he would become. In his early film *Blonde Venus* (1932), with Marlene

Dietrich, Grant has a sinister side, and in a series of Mae West films Grant played the innocent. It was not until *The Awful Truth* in 1937 that Grant found his debonair persona. Like most stars, Grant's image was carefully crafted, and it remained coherent even as he worked in different genres and enjoyed ongoing collaborations with some of the most distinctive directors in Hollywood, including Alfred Hitchcock, George Cukor, and Howard Hawks.

Grant's offscreen persona complemented the dapper demeanor and charmed life he led onscreen. Fan magazines reported on Grant's glamorous nightlife and multiple marriages to costars and socialites. Stars' high profile relationships would often develop into popular press soap operas on their own, part real, part studio publicity, and part public fantasy. When Grant married Woolworth heiress Barbara Hutton, for example, the press began to refer contemptuously to the made-for-publicity couple as "Cash and Cary." It was a precursor to the later celebrity relationships worthy of their own names like Brangelina (Brad Pitt and Angelina Jolie), Bennifer (Ben Affleck and Jennifer Lopez), and TomKat (Tom Cruise and Katie Holmes).

Reporting on stars' personal lives often allowed for multiple and contradictory interpretations of their star persona. Photos of Grant exercising with his longtime roommate Randolph Scott, for example, could reinforce the image of them as playboys or stir speculation about Grant's bisexuality. Either way, the carefully curated images brought in more devoted fans.

Whatever fans saw and read in newspapers they took with them into the next film. Studios carefully constructed star images, producing their own fan magazines, training stars for public appearances, and in many cases even orchestrating stars' private lives. As a result, audiences could not help but watch movie stars with double vision, as both the part they played in a particular film and as the star persona that developed offscreen and across films. The studios counted on this dual vision to anchor

4. Studio publicity departments used images that appealed to multiple publics. Photos of longtime roommates Cary Grant and Randolph Scott portrayed the active lifestyle of the two screen heartthrobs, but the images could also be interpreted as showing them as a couple.

the unpredictable successes and failures of individual films in the consistency of the star system.

There is no better evidence of the value of stars than the animated films of the 1930s, 1940s, and 1950s. Disney had Mickey and

Minnie Mouse, Donald Duck, and Pluto, while Warner Bros. had Bugs Bunny, Daffy Duck, and Elmer Fudd. The star system became so important to making, marketing, and consuming movies that even animated movies needed stars to build audience loyalty and character recognition.

During the classical studio era, stars were closely associated with a studio's house style as well, because stars were generally long-term studio employees. They were under contract to a single studio for five to seven years and worked forty weeks a year with twelve weeks of unpaid vacation. Even top-billed stars had very little say about the roles that they were assigned.

As production heads came up with a plan for the year's slate of films, they chose projects around their stable of stars. And if a star was not needed, he or she could be loaned out to another studio, often at a very high price. In rare cases, top stars had one loan-out a year built into their contracts, so that they could pursue artistic ambitions. But lending out a star could help the home studio as well. When MGM loaned Clark Gable to Columbia Pictures to make Frank Capra's *It Happened One Night* (1934), Gable won an Oscar and came back to MGM more bankable than ever. The loan was also beneficial to Columbia, which had a top director, Capra, but a modest stable of actors.

In the 1930s, a few stars, including Fred Astaire, Cary Grant, Carole Lombard, and Ginger Rogers, were able to remain successful as freelancers, liberated from long studio contracts. But they were the exceptions. Stars, for the most part, were tied to an individual studio and remained an essential part of that studio's identity.

As stars' celebrity grew, so did their power in the studio system. In the mid-1910s, Chaplin and Mary Pickford were able to convert their audience draw into lucrative salaries and creative autonomy. Chaplin built his own studio, and Pickford shared in the profits from her films as early as 1915 (although many histories claim incorrectly that Jimmy Stewart was the first star to get profit-sharing "points" for his role in *Winchester '73* (1950). In 1919 Chaplin and Pickford teamed up with Douglas Fairbanks and director D. W. Griffith to start United Artists, which served as a distributor for independent production companies before becoming a full-fledged studio itself.

During the height of the constricting contact system in the 1930s, several of the most successful stars fought for more control over their own careers, including Bette Davis, Myrna Loy, and James Cagney, who all lost battles with their respective studios. It was Olivia de Havilland, frustrated with repetitive ingénue roles, who successfully took on the studios and won some rights for her peers, at great personal expense. In 1946, de Havilland thought she had completed her seven-year contract with Warner Bros. But the studio informed her that an additional six months had been added on to compensate for periods when she had turned down roles and not been actively working—a common studio practice. De Havilland sued the studio and won in California's Supreme Court, which decided that her contract lasted for seven years regardless of whether she was shooting a film or not. It was an important victory, both legally and symbolically, demonstrating that actors could no longer be treated like the property of the studios. It also showed the strength of the Screen Actors Guild, the actors' union incorporated in 1933, which supported de Havilland. The victory proved to be costly for de Havilland, however. In retribution the studios refused to hire her for two years.

The genre system

Stars bring consistency to filmmaking and filmgoing; genres bring order. Throughout the history of Hollywood, westerns, musicals, and other genres have been important to all aspects of film production, distribution, marketing, exhibition, and consumption. Genres breed familiarity by standardizing storytelling, offering formulas for defining characters, and controlling viewers' expectations. Genres also provide a vocabulary for inserting political meaning into film—even a small change in a genre movie can have large repercussions for how the film is interpreted by audiences and critics.

Of course genres preceded movies. There are genres of painting, theater, literature, and music, many of which migrated to film. Yet it is difficult to articulate an adequate definition of genre or even to define a specific genre. Many different elements make up a genre, some or all of which can be present in a specific film. Settings, iconography, narrative patterns, and aesthetic styles are just some of the ingredients that make up a genre. Westerns can be identified by their prairie, ranch, or frontier-town locations. Zombies or vampires indicate that we are watching a horror movie. All that is needed to make a film a comedy is a light attitude or ironic tone. And films noirs are characterized by high-contrast lighting and femmes fatales characters, if indeed film noir is a genre and not an aesthetic style or historical period, as critics have debated. To make matters more complicated, a single film can mix genres, such as the longstanding comic-horror genre, which stretches from *Abbott and Costello Meet Frankenstein* (1948) to *Young Frankenstein* (1974) to *Scary Movie 3* (2003).

During the classical studio period, the 1910s–1960s, genres were closely tied to both house styles and the star system, and it is impossible to determine which component of the studio system led the others. Warner Bros. specialized in gangster films in the 1930s, creating an identity for the studio. The genre appealed to the studio's working-class urban audience and made use of its tough male stars such as James Cagney, Humphrey Bogart, and John Garfield.

In the 1930s, Universal Studios became known for a successful run of horror films, starting with *Frankenstein* (1931), *Dracula* (1931), and *The Old Dark House* (1932). The Universal horror cycle adapted popular plays, and it employed the production design, lighting, and cinematography that German émigré filmmakers trained in the expressionist style brought with them to Hollywood. Universal horror became one of the best-known studio genre brands. Although genres became part of studios' identities, no studio claimed exclusive rights to any one genre. Every studio made musicals and westerns, and when one studio had a breakaway hit with a genre film, the other studios invariably jumped in with their own follow-up film.

The star system, too, was deeply intertwined with the genre system. The early success of westerns in the 1900s was among the factors that drove production from New York City to Fort Lee, New Jersey, and eventually west to Los Angeles in search of rugged terrain and sunshine. Westerns also called for iconic heroes and villains, and many of the early male stars rose to prominence as distinctly western stars, including William S. Hart, Tom Mix, Roy Rogers, and Gene Autry. The iconicity of both the hero and the star overlapped perfectly and reinforced each other. Some stars became so closely identified with particular genres that they were typecast, unable to break out of their defined role. John Wayne made westerns. Fred Astaire and Ginger Rogers made musicals. Errol Flynn made costume dramas. Esther Williams was restricted almost entirely to aquatic ballet musicals.

Like stars, producers and directors became associated with genres, and the structure of the studios revolved around genre production. Units within studios were devoted entirely to making romantic comedies or westerns. Producer Val Lewton ran the horror unit at RKO. At Warner Bros., director William Dieterle specialized in biographical films (a genre later dubbed the biopic) starring Paul Muni, and MGM's Freed Unit became famous for making some of the most successful musicals of the classical studio era.

Under the direction of lyricist-turned-producer Arthur Freed, the Freed Unit employed top songwriting teams, including Richard Rodgers–Lorenz Hart and Betty Comden–Adolph Green. At different times, the Freed Unit also included singing and dancing stars Gene Kelly, Lena Horne, Cyd Charisse, and Frank Sinatra.

The Freed Unit's commercial and artistic success owed much to its novel approach to the musical genre. The problem that all musicals seek to overcome is how to incorporate music into everyday life in a way that audiences will find believable (or at least not laughable). Musicals frequently explain all the singing and dancing by using a backstage musical plot, the most common subgenre. Everyone is singing because they are putting on a show. In other musicals, there is a pause, music swells up on the soundtrack, and the characters burst into song. Freed aimed for a more integrated approach to music and dancing. First, Freed Unit musicals contain what Freed called a "thesis," which explains why a character will break into song, and, second, the song is essential to the plot. The narrative does not come to a halt, making way for a musical number; the number advances the story.

Director Vincente Minnelli's 1944 Freed Unit musical *Meet Me in St. Louis*, for example, contains a trolley car scene with a clear thesis. The film's star, Judy Garland, boards a trolley as it clangs along and the conductor dings the bell. The vehicle is almost musical, and indeed the rhythm and noise of the trolley begin to mingle with music on the soundtrack. Garland starts to feel her love for a boy swell inside her, and she begins to explain in a half talking, half singing voice that she "went to lose a jolly hour on the trolley and lost [her] heart instead." Then she states the thesis clearly:

> Clang, clang, clang went the trolley
> Ding, ding, ding went the bell
> Zing, zing, zing went my heartstrings
> From the moment I saw him I fell.

The musical sounds of the trolley mirror the rhythm of her heart. That metaphorical thesis is the springboard for a song, and the musical number is seamlessly integrated into the narrative and action of the scene.

The Freed Unit tweaked the musical formula, but providing storytelling formulas is the primary function of genres. Genres offer premade characters, settings, tensions, endings, and subplots. A producer can turn to a writer, as the fictional producer does in *Barton Fink* (1991), the Coen brothers' movie about Hollywood history, and say, "We're gonna put you to work on a wrestling picture." And the writer (like the audience) should already know exactly what to expect from the movie. When the producer tells Barton Fink that the wrestling movie will star Wallace Beery, the brawny real-life star of such films as *The Champ* (1931), the writer should have all of the elements needed to construct the main character and plot. Indeed, the pleasure of watching movie stars and genre films is not discovering how the film will end. We already know that the hero will triumph (or die if it is a tragedy). The pleasure comes from watching the complications that defer the ending and alter the narrative formula we are familiar with.

Moreover, every tiny alteration to a heist plot or an alien-invasion film is an opportunity for a writer or director to stamp the film with his or her authorial mark and make a statement about society. The reuse of the same plots in genre films makes them into rituals, like fables and bedtime stories, that reflect the times in which they are told. And small changes to the expected formula speak volumes.

In *The Man Who Shot Liberty Valance* (1962), director John Ford self-consciously calls attention to many of the tropes of the western while simultaneously looking out to American culture of the early 1960s. It is a film with two heroes. One is Tom Doniphon, a tough rancher played by John Wayne. The other is a frail lawyer, Ransom Stoddard, played by Jimmy Stewart. The film plays out their competing approaches to bringing civilization to the wilderness of the American West. Stoddard supports democratic institutions: the press, the school, and the rule of law. Doniphon claims that only violence gets results. Doniphon clearly represents a fading approach to law and order in the west, while Stoddard points to the future.

In the end, the story and the film's message culminate with a three-person shoot-out involving Doniphon, Stoddard, and the villain terrorizing the town, Liberty Valance (Lee Marvin). And—spoiler alert—both heroes are proven right. The villain Liberty Valance is shot. At first it appears that Stoddard has killed Valance in self-defense, and, based on that one act of bravery, Stoddard goes on to win a seat in the US Senate and bring law and order to the state. We learn in a flashback, however, that it was really Doniphon who shot Valance, while hiding in the shadows. Cold-blooded murder, not justified self-defense, led to Stoddard's political rise. Violence, the film suggests, is the necessary foundation for the institutions of civilization. And we need our wild heroes just as much as we need our political leaders.

The Man Who Shot Liberty Valance sets up a classic western plot point: the shoot-out. By repeating the scene, Ford shows us how the staging of the shoot-out can lead to different interpretations of the film and society. Ford trains his audience to read the meaning of the smallest genre details. The film also contains not so oblique references to the civil rights movement and the Cold War, just in case audiences missed the film's relevance to contemporary politics.

Genre films like *The Man Who Shot Liberty Valance* serve an allegorical function, retelling stories in ways that reflect back on society. And the more successful genre films are the ones that connect with the fears and concerns of audiences. For that reason, genres generally appear in cycles. We often hear that westerns, musicals, or other genres have died out and lost their relevance, only to see them return in new cycles that reimagine the genres for a new time.

The 1990s, for example, saw independently made westerns with black (*Posse*, 1993), female (*Ballad of Little Jo*, 1993), and, later, gay (*Brokeback Mountain*, 2005) heroes, inserting greater diversity into American national mythology. Westerns, in particular, remain important, because they symbolize the always new social and political frontiers of American society. And genre films retain their power, because they turn filmgoing into a ritual. Audiences go to genre movies for a communal retelling of familiar narratives, reading for meaning in the details.

Chapter 3
Sound and the Production Code

Despite studio heads' best efforts to manage risk and build consistency into the studio system, they have never been able to stave off disruptions for very long. There is always a new cultural, aesthetic, or technological change on the horizon. The studios have not always responded to these disruptions in the same way, yet Hollywood has consistently managed to adjust to new circumstances. And in almost every instance, the studio system has emerged stronger than it was before the change.

Sound and the challenges of new technology

The move to synchronized sound cinema was arguably the largest format shift in the history of moving images. To switch from one digital format to another simply requires a software conversion. But the adoption of sound required every studio and every theater to be refitted with new sound technology and sound-friendly architecture. In part for that reason, Hollywood was slow to adopt synchronized sound, and, in a pattern that is repeated throughout film history, the smaller studios led the way forward.

Edison had plans to combine sound and image even in his first experiments. And German, French, and English inventors developed synchronized sound systems throughout the 1910s and 1920s. The American inventor Lee DeForest developed one of the most successful early sound-film technologies, called Phonofilm. DeForest had been a key inventor of radio technology, and he perfected his sound-film technology in the early 1920s. Phonofilm used a sound-on-film system, converting sound waves into light waves, which were then printed on film next to the images. It was an effective method of keeping sound and image in synchronization, and DeForest promoted his invention with films of many celebrities, including comedian Eddie Cantor and President Calvin Coolidge.

Phonofilm premiered at the Rivoli Theatre in New York in 1923. The animation team of Max and Dave Fleischer were excited by the display, and they made a series of short films using Phonofilm. But no major studio licensed the technology, and DeForest became embroiled in patent disputes that bogged down his company. In the end, his invention foundered largely because it was slightly ahead of his time. It would be another two or three years before all of the financial pieces were in place for studios to begin experimenting with sound.

When sound did come to Hollywood, two then-minor studios, Warner Bros. and Fox, pursued the new technology as part of ultimately successful expansion bids. Paramount, MGM, and other major studios owned large theater chains and had flagship movie palaces in major cities where their films were shown with live music. Warner Bros. initially planned to make sound shorts to show between feature films, replicating the feeling of having live entertainment.

Fox's scheme entailed moving slowly into sound film by adding voice-overs to newsreels. Both studios also took out large loans, built extensive sound stages, and invested in theaters as well. Warner Bros. bought a radio station to promote its new sound division, and Fox bought the Roxy movie palace in New York, so that it would have a first-run theater.

The two companies bet on very different technologies. Warner Bros. teamed up with Western Electric/AT&T and investment bank Goldman Sachs to create a sound-on-disc technology called Vitaphone. As a movie played, it was synchronized with a record. Fox licensed US and German patents to create a sound-on-film technology called Movietone, which had much better synchronization than Vitaphone. Together, they started a format war. Few theaters could afford to adopt multiple sound formats, and if one company controlled film sound technology, it would have a major competitive advantage.

In 1926–1927, both Warner Bros. and Fox moved into sound-film production. They made shorts, newsreels, and feature films with synchronized music tracks. Many of these experiments showed off what sound could do for the film experience. One Fox Movietone short featured playwright George Bernard Shaw casually strolling up to the camera and offering a seemingly off-the-cuff monologue. The short is carefully framed and scripted to give the audience the impression that they are having a personal encounter with a celebrity. The addition of synchronized sound makes the experience all the more immediate. There is one jarring moment, however, at the very end. Shaw says "goodnight" and then realizes that his audience might be watching a matinee in which case, he points out, he should have said "good afternoon." The slip breaks the illusion and reminds both Shaw and viewers of the mediated nature of the encounter. But it also reminds us just how transporting the film had been up until that point. In the 1920s, the film created a powerful feeling of proximity to a well-known figure; today it brings a long-dead literary giant back to life.

In other experiments, Warner Bros. and Fox recorded lush orchestral scores and some minor sound effects to be synchronized with feature-length films. The first Vitaphone feature, *Don Juan* (1926), starred John Barrymore in Warner Bros.' most expensive production up until that time. Sparing no expense, the studio hired the New York Philharmonic to record the score. In many theaters, *Don Juan* was preceded by a short film of Hollywood's chief spokesperson, Will Hays, promoting the new phenomenon of sound film.

Synchronized soundtracks represented a significant change in the creative power dynamics of the film industry. Filmgoing had always been a partially local experience. Silent films arrived at theaters incomplete, and exhibitors were left to add music and sometimes sound effects, which could be as much a part of the show as the images. Starting in the mid-1910s, film producers began sending musical scores to accompany films, but not every theater could accommodate producers' requests, and the exhibitors could easily ignore the printed scores. The addition of synchronized soundtracks, however, consolidated creative control in the hands of producers, who now oversaw every aspect of the film experience. Film took the final step in becoming a mass medium.

It is sometimes claimed that the introduction of sound set the visual art of moviemaking back years. Virtuosic late silent films like William Wellman's *Wings* (1927) and King Vidor's *The Crowd* (1928) gave way to stilted early sound productions with stationary cameras and equally stationary actors, who needed to stay close to on-set microphones—a situation later satirized in *Singin' in the Rain* (1952).

But many of the earliest sound films brought the art of radio and theater to the movies. One early sound classic began when William Fox hired German expressionist director F. W. Murnau to make a prestige silent movie, to which a synchronized Movietone soundtrack was later added. Murnau took two popular Fox contract stars, Janet Gaynor and George O'Brien, and put them in a moody expressionistic masterpiece, *Sunrise* (1927).

In *Sunrise*, Gaynor and O'Brien play the Man and the Wife, a country couple who have marital problems when O'Brien has an affair with the Woman from the City. The city woman convinces O'Brien to drown his wife, but when he takes Gaynor out on a boat, he cannot go through with the murder. O'Brien furiously rows the boat to the city shore, and the couple spend the day wandering through the city while their love is rekindled. In the style of German expressionist films, which were still in fashion in the United States, the film explores the characters' internal states of mind in addition to the objective reality of the narrative.

The soundtrack is as powerful a force as the images. In a pivotal scene, for example, Gaynor and O'Brien happen upon a wedding in progress. They hear the church bells ring and are reminded of their own vows. Wandering from the church into an intersection, the couple embarks on a collective reverie: they are visually transported back to country, and we see them walking into a meadow. The soundtrack also relates their emotional experience of the moment, and we hear the leitmotif associated with the country sequences from earlier in the film. All of a sudden, the reality that traffic has descended upon them in the busy intersection is signaled first by horns and men yelling on the soundtrack. Then they are shown surrounded by cars and trucks. The music and sound effects mix the interior and exterior experiences of the characters, creating an early work of subjective sound artistry.

Sunrise may be a classic of film history, but at the time of its release it was upstaged by the two short films that accompanied its premiere. A film of the Vatican choir demonstrated that sound film could bring the best of the world's music to theaters everywhere, while a film showing a speech by Benito Mussolini brought current events to life.

Sunrise was also buried under the excitement for *The Jazz Singer* (1927), which Warner Bros. released just two weeks later. *The Jazz Singer* is famous as the first talkie, but both technically and aesthetically it is a strange object. It is a patchwork of sound and silent cinema, theater and movies, all wrapped in the blackface minstrel tradition, which was already in decline. At some level, this works with the plot, which is about the clash of traditions. The main character, played by Broadway star Al Jolson, leaves the cantorial tradition of his Jewish family to sing jazz. But the mix of styles also feels like Warner Bros. was taking only the tiniest step toward real sound cinema. *The Jazz Singer* is essentially a silent movie with a few musical interludes, some of which contain talking before or after a song.

The film had to be released in fifteen separate reels, each with its own disc, to give projectionists the best chance of keeping all of the scenes in synchronization. Many filmgoers had seen talking and musical shorts before *The Jazz Singer*, and the film is really just a series of musical shorts integrated into a silent feature film. But that was enough to suggest the possibilities of all-talking-and-singing movies, and *The Jazz Singer* hastened the revolution already in progress.

The leaders of the five major studios at the time—First National, MGM, Paramount, Producers Distributing Corporation, and Universal—watched from the sidelines as Fox and Warner Bros. fought their format war. The studio heads realized that if any one company controlled the sound platform, it would have too much power. Eight months before *The Jazz Singer*'s premiere, the majors signed a formal agreement among themselves saying that they would study the options and all adopt a single sound standard. Eventually, the studios all transitioned to a new sound-on-film technology developed by Western Electric.

For a few years, studios released films in multiple formats, but by 1930 the transition to a single sound format was complete. The disruption unleashed by two smaller companies reshuffled the makeup of the industry: there were new mergers and reorganizations, and one entirely new studio, RKO, was started. But in the end, the introduction of sound strengthened Hollywood.

Largely because sound made film into an exciting novelty, the American film industry was one of the few—if not the only—industry to prosper during the first years of the Great Depression. The effects of the Depression on Hollywood were delayed because of sound, but they did hit eventually, and every studio with the exception of MGM experienced significant financial problems in the early 1930s. Among other issues, the stock market crash shortly after the studios took out large loans to support their conversion to sound ended up increasing Wall Street's control of the movie industry.

Of course sound had major aesthetic implications as well. Silent film had been an international language. With the translation of a few title cards, films could be shown in any country. But sound film turned movie production into a monolingual enterprise. At first, studios tried shooting films in multiple languages with multiple casts. The English-speaking actors shot a scene, and then the Spanish-speaking actors took their turn, followed by French-speaking cast. But that expensive and cumbersome solution did not last long. By the early 1930s dubbing and subtitling facilities had been set up in most major export markets.

There was also a bit of truth to the claims that sound cinema set filmmaking back. Early sound technology imposed many technical and artistic constraints on studio productions. Noisy cameras needed to be confined to immobile soundproof booths, so that the mechanical sounds of the camera would not interfere with the recording. Actors were recorded live on set, and they had to stand close to the large microphones concealed by scenery or hanging from the studio rafters. Sometimes whole orchestras were placed on the set to provide background music, because for a time musical scores could not be added after shooting. And long scenes needed to be recorded in one take to avoid disruptive sound cuts.

Limited by the technology, in the late 1920s and early 1930s Hollywood lured writers, singers, and stage performers to Los

Angeles to provide the dialogue and music needed for sound movies. They churned out musicals and dramas that were little more than filmed theater. But sometimes not knowing the technical limitation can be a path to innovation. It took a theater director, Rouben Mamoulian, making his first film, *Applause* (1929), to free the camera again. He put the large soundproof camera booths on wheels, and he recorded multiple sound tracks that were mixed together during postproduction. And Hollywood successfully incorporated sound technology into both the business and art of the studio system.

The Production Code

Hollywood's transition to sound came during turbulent times. In addition to the Great Depression, the 1930s saw the rise of fascist and communist world powers, and in the United States longstanding complaints by religious organizations that Hollywood was inciting violence and immorality reached a fever pitch. The Hollywood studios ultimately addressed all of these issues by adopting the Production Code. The Production Code is widely misunderstood as a form of censorship. It is more accurate to see it as document that helped the industry frame political and social messages and reach a broad audience.

Pressure on the American film industry to regulate its content began early. Edison's trust, the Motion Picture Patents Company, as we saw earlier, adopted a form of self-censorship in order to deflect criticism and government regulation. Despite the trust's efforts, however, many state censor boards arose to control the distribution of film in the United States. In 1915, the Mutual Film Corporation challenged the Ohio state censor board in a case that eventually reached the Supreme Court. In a unanimous decision, the court ruled that filmmakers were not entitled to freedom of speech under the First Amendment. On the contrary, the decision declared the movie industry to be "a business pure and simple," and stated further that films are "capable of evil." The decision went on to worry about the mixing of men and women, children and adults in the public space of the movie theater. Rather than a form of creative expression, film would be treated like meat or industrial waste, regulated for the health of society. State censorship of film was officially sanctioned, and films would not enjoy First Amendment protection until the 1950s.

One type of federal film-content regulation followed quickly on the heels of the Mutual decision. During World War I, journalist George Creel oversaw the Committee on Public Information, a propaganda organization established by President Woodrow Wilson. Among other tasks, the Creel Committee, as it was called, lobbied for legislation to put the circulation of American media in the service of the war. The Espionage Act of 1917 banned media that interfered with military operations and recruitment; the Trading with the Enemy Act, passed the same year, allowed government oversight of all exported media; and the Sedition Act of 1918 broadly outlawed disloyal statements.

These were not idle pieces of legislation. One filmmaker served three years of a ten-year sentence for making a film that depicted British atrocities during the American Revolutionary War. The film, the court decided, would strain relations with US ally Britain. The repercussions of the Espionage Act continue to be felt, and it has been used in the twenty-first century to prosecute government employees who have leaked confidential information, including Chelsea (formerly Bradley) Manning and Edward Snowden. Outside of the United States in the 1910s and 1920s, many countries had censorship policies that applied to US exported films, and the United Kingdom adopted a rating system.

In addition to government oversight, Hollywood felt pressure from religious leaders whose indignation was fueled by a succession of Hollywood scandals. First, two of America's biggest stars, Mary Pickford and Douglas Fairbanks, married each other while Pickford's quickie divorce from her first husband was still being contested. Then, matinee idol Wallace Reid died as a result of his morphine addiction. But the most damaging scandal involved the murder trial of popular comedian Fatty Arbuckle. Arbuckle was accused of the rape and murder of actress Virginia Rappe during a party at the St. Francis Hotel in San Francisco. After three trials, Arbuckle was acquitted, but the manslaughter charge was not the real scandal. Newspaper readers were titillated and shocked by the salacious details of wild Hollywood parties that came out during the protracted trials.

In order to counter pressure from religious groups and the looming threat of federal film censorship, the studios formed the Motion Picture Producers and Distributors of America (MPPDA), which later became the Motion Picture Association of America. Major League Baseball had similarly addressed its corruption scandals a few years earlier by appointing a commissioner to clean up the industry.

The MPPDA's head, Will Hays, was not only a well-connected Republican Party leader; he was also an awkward-looking Presbyterian elder. In other words, he embodied the opposite of Hollywood's glamorous, indulgent image. Under Hays's leadership, the MPPDA collaborated with Protestant and Catholic leaders to construct a set of guidelines for the film industry. They wrote a preliminary draft in 1924, which became the list of "Don'ts and Be Carefuls" in 1927, which was finally formalized as the Production Code in 1930.

The code listed general principles to be followed, as well as some specific no-nos. It acknowledged that Hollywood had a moral and political obligation to its audience, but it also defended filmmakers' need to depict some "evil" in the service of drama. Filmmakers were warned not to depict sex and crime "alluringly," and films were never to ridicule religion, celebrate obscenity (the can-can dance was listed as an example) or represent non-Americans unfavorably. In other words, the code ensured that films would not take controversial political or moral positions, and, as a result, Hollywood would avoid offending potential ticket buyers in the United States and abroad. Finally, the code contained story-writing advice, helping to achieve the always present goal of imposing filmmaking formulas.

The Production Code made it clear that sex, violence, and political extremism were often necessary for movie plots, but they needed to be contained within a narrative that clearly signaled a mainstream moral and political center. Extramarital sex, for example, had to be appropriately punished, usually by death. Criminals could engage in violence as long as they paid the price later. It has been said that if you lop off the last twenty minutes of all American movies, Hollywood would have the most transgressive cinema tradition in the world. If that is true, it is largely as a result of filmmakers appeasing the MPPDA by using narratives designed to reveal and then contain sex, violence, and politics.

The first thing that Hollywood did after establishing the code in 1930 was to ignore it, and 1930-1933 is known, confusingly, as the "precode era." Instead of reining in filmmakers, the code ushered in a period of sexually explicit, violent, and politically revolutionary movies. During the precode era, screenwriter and actress Mae West delighted in devising novel double entendres, violent gangster films flourished, and filmmakers flirted with fascism and communism.

One of the stranger films of the period, *Gabriel over the White House* (1933), was independently produced by Hollywood insider Walter Wanger and newspaper magnate William Randolph Hearst and distributed by MGM. The film melds fascist and socialist ideologies to imagine a US president who assumes dictatorial control over the country in order to implement a system of social services, much like those proposed at the time by Democratic presidential contender Franklin Delano Roosevelt. MGM head and ardent Republican Louis B. Mayer wanted the film permanently shelved. But its release was ultimately delayed until after Roosevelt's inauguration to lessen the relevance of its radical message. Indeed, many precode films were so risqué that when they were rereleased, they had to be recut to meet the stricter moral standards of the late 1930s, 1940s, or 1950s.

The precode era may seem like a period with little oversight by the MPPDA, but the code was actively being enforced at the time by the organization's Studio Relations Committee (SRC), overseen by longtime MPPDA employee Jason Joy. The Production Code files contain thousands of letters between the SRC and the studios discussing script ideas, plot details, and completed films. The SRC stayed closely involved with all studio productions during the period, and every film released by the studios received a seal saying that it had passed the SRC's scrutiny.

In general, the SRC took a two-pronged approach to ensuring films met its standards. First, the SRC attempted to minimize the spectacle of sexually explicit, violent, or politically controversial material. Films could not show too much. And second, as dictated by the code, the SRC made sure that when such spectacles were important to the plot, they were explained through narratives that punished the wicked and reinforced the effectiveness of social institutions like the police and the courts.

One slightly unusual example of a film that went through the SRC oversight process is *Scarface* (1932), a film produced by wealthy eccentric businessman Howard Hughes, who went on to have a long history of pushing the boundaries of the Production Code. *Scarface* was the loosely fictionalized story of real-life gangster Al Capone. Capone shared the nicknamed Scarface with the film's title character, and he bore a close physical resemblance to the film's star, Paul Muni. The SRC opposed this film from the start, both because of its extreme violence and because the SRC feared that it would glamourize gangsters, making Capone into a hero. But Hughes and director Howard Hawks could not be deterred. They continued to push back against SRC warnings until they convinced Jason Joy that the film's excessive violence added up to a condemnation of violence.

The SRC may have been convinced of the film's pacifist message, but they wanted to ensure that audiences received that message correctly too. First, the SRC required a subtitle *Scarface: The Shame of the Nation*. Then they inserted a long printed prologue, explaining that the film represented the threat of violence to American society, and it was a call for Congress to solve the problem. Finally, the SRC had alternate endings shot by a new director. The original film ends with Scarface surviving what should have been a fatal barrage of gunshots. Brian DePalma's 1983 remake with Al Pacino ends similarly, though Pacino is finally killed.

In the first alternate ending, Scarface begs for mercy when he finds himself cornered by the police, revealing that, underneath the tough exterior he displayed throughout the film, he was cowardly in the face of death, deterring children who might idolize him. In the second alternate ending, Scarface is sentenced to death and executed, reinforcing the power of state institutions to cure society's ailments. The SRC believed that the narrative frame contained the controversial spectacle of violence that Scarface displays throughout the film, and Jason Joy and Will Hays lobbied state censor boards—often unsuccessfully—for permission to show the film.

It is important to remember that the SRC worked for the studios. It was Joy and Hays's job to help films sail smoothly past state and foreign censor boards, reaching more ticket buyers. The Production Code enforcers were not the final arbiters of morality; they were the intermediaries, trying to ensure that Hollywood reflected mainstream morality and ideology.

By 1933, it became clear that the SRC was not sufficiently quelling the growing wave of anti-Hollywood criticism. A series of dubious academic studies, known collectively as the Payne Fund studies, sought to prove that film violence led to a more violent society. Despite heavy academic criticism, the studies resulted in several books and many newspaper headlines. The research was eventually summarized in a popular and inflammatory book, *Our Movie-Made Children* (1935).

In 1933 religious opposition to Hollywood came to a new head as well with the formation of the Catholic Legion of Decency, dedicated to purifying the American film industry and later rating films. The organization quickly expanded to include a wider range of religious leaders. Also, by that time, the Depression had hit Hollywood, ticket sales were down, and the studios were more vulnerable than ever to institutionalized opposition to movies.

In response to the chorus of critics, the MPPDA rebranded the SRC the Production Code Administration (PCA). Jason Joy was replaced by Joseph Breen, who adopted a new approach to applying the code. Breen embraced the job with the zeal of a true believer, and his notorious anti-Semitism and staunch anticommunist beliefs stoked his hatred of Hollywood. Breen brought a more systematic approach to film regulation, and he introduced stricter standards.

Even with Breen's censorial attitude, however, the Production Code remained a studio-biased document, designed to help sell more films. The PCA continued to offer expertise on the standards of state and foreign censor boards, advising Hollywood screenwriters, for example, not to include the word "lousy," which was fine in the United States but not permitted in the United Kingdom, where it retained its original meaning and suggested the presence of lice. Breen also took extra care to prevent studios from offending politicians in Washington whom the industry might later need to call on for a favor.

Like the star and genre systems, the Production Code brought standardization to the business of filmmaking. It also helped codify the language of storytelling, developing a system of representation that could be read in multiple ways. This multivalent language applied to dialogue, editing, acting, and cinematography. As Jason Joy once put it, the studios and the Production Code enforcers collaborated to create a language "from which conclusions might be drawn by the sophisticated mind, but which would mean nothing to the unsophisticated and inexperienced."

It might be more accurate to say that Hollywood bifurcated its audience into spectators who chose—consciously or not—to read cues one way or another. We all know that a couple kissing followed by a pan to a fireplace implies that their offscreen activity is heating up. But that is only the most cliché example of the system of double meanings Hollywood and the MPPDA created to allow films to address complex issues during the golden age of the studios.

Josef von Sternberg's precode melodrama *Blonde Venus* (1932), for example, led to a very long correspondence between the director and the SRC as they negotiated how to tell the story of a woman who uses sex to advance her singing career in an attempt to pay for her sick husband's medical care. In the second half of the film, Helen, played by Marlene Dietrich, is forced to work as a prostitute. After very heavy editing, however, there are only a few hints to suggest her career change. The most explicit reference comes when Helen is unable to pay for her dinner at a restaurant, and the owner offers a barter of sex with the phrase, "You gonna wash my dishes?" In the context of the narrative, it is not hard to catch the suggested meaning. But audiences could understand it literally if they chose to.

5. Cary Grant, Katharine Hepburn, May Robson, and Asta (the dog) on the set of *Bringing Up Baby* (RKO, 1938). Grant is dressed in the outfit he wears when he skirts the Production Code with the line "I just went gay all of a sudden."

The Production Code's multivalent language worked with other elements of the studio system. Just as Cary Grant's offscreen star image could be crafted to be read as both straight and gay, so could his onscreen image. And, of course, the two images reinforced each other. Even though representations of homosexuality, or "sex perversion," as it was called in the Production Code, were officially banned by the SRC and PCA, queerness could be suggested in many ways. When, for example, a woman walks through a door in Howard Hawks's *Bringing Up Baby* (1938) to find Grant in a frilly woman's dressing gown, she asks why he is dressed that way. Grant jumps up exuberantly and declares, "Because I just went gay all of a sudden." At the time, the word gay perfectly fit Hollywood's developing double language. Its dominant meaning was still happy, but gay was also starting to connote homosexuality, and that reading was available to some audience members, especially if they had read about Grant's offscreen life. Grant's line was also an ad lib, not in the original script, and so would have avoided the script stage of PCA scrutiny. It is a testament to the openness of the code that today both meanings have switched, and the minority of viewers will hear gay to mean happy.

At first it may seem shocking that an industry would regulate itself so heavily. But upon closer inspection it becomes clear that the Production Code served an integral role in the standardization of the studio system, reducing the risks that films might find opposition along the distribution chain. It kept US federal and religious censors at bay; it smoothed films' paths through state and foreign censor boards; it codified film stories with a set of narrative expectations; and it created a language for obliquely addressing sex, violence, and politics. Rather than a restrictive set of rules, the Production Code was a framework for Hollywood to take on otherwise taboo subjects. And, not to be underestimated, the Production Code helped sell more tickets.

Chapter 4
Hollywood at war

President Franklin Delano Roosevelt ran for reelection in 1940 on an isolationist platform; he promised to keep the United States out of what many called "the European war." But when Japan bombed the Pearl Harbor naval base in Hawaii on December 7, 1941, public sentiment changed, and the United States entered World War II. Over the next year, FDR established the Bureau of Motion Pictures and a number of additional offices and agencies designed to enlist Hollywood in the war effort. Further enticing Hollywood to collaborate with the US military, the Department of Justice agreed to suspend an ongoing antitrust investigation of the studios, and the Selective Service System declared Hollywood to be an essential industry, exempting its critical personnel from the draft.

The film studios signed on to help fight the war, using movies and star power to shape public opinion. Even beyond direct government work, Hollywood contributed to the larger war effort by making patriotic films, raising money for war bonds, and entertaining troops. It has been estimated that as much as one-third of Hollywood production during the war directly bolstered America's wartime activities, and, not coincidentally, it was also one of the most profitable stretches in Hollywood's history. The film industry, the moviegoing public, and the country were all in sync for a time.

Hollywood gets political

FDR's fascination with Hollywood and popular media long predated the war. He had ties to Hollywood as far back as his days as governor of New York. After becoming president, FDR regularly invited actors, directors, and studio heads to the White House. He screened several films a week for family and friends. And he transferred his love of film to his son, James, who had an undistinguished career as a Hollywood producer before serving in the Marines and then in Congress. Not only did FDR love film; he mastered the art of using film and radio to shape public opinion. He became famous for his "fireside chats," radio addresses that personalized his political agenda and always began with the intimate salutation "My friends."

The Roosevelt administration also used documentary films in the 1930s to explain its New Deal policies, producing such masterpieces of the genre as *The Plow That Broke the Plains* (1936) and *The River* (1938). And the New Deal workers' relief project, the Works Progress Administration, employed many writers, directors, and actors who would go on to have distinguished Hollywood careers, including Orson Welles, Nicholas Ray, and Sidney Lumet. Really showing his media savvy, FDR decided to appoint as the first White House press secretary Stephen Early, the Washington representative for Paramount Pictures' newsreel service. FDR valued the American film industry, and the relationship went both ways. The president enjoyed broad support in Hollywood, even from right-wing stalwarts like Jack Warner.

FDR's interest in the media dovetailed with the film industry's turn toward politics, and Hollywood was primed for war when the time came. The film community had been far ahead of the country as a whole in calling for intervention in the war, and many of the industry's leaders were already deeply engaged in European politics.

On a business level, wartime hostilities closed off some European markets, which contributed to the studios' diminishing attention to the needs of European audiences. And slowly, the move toward war overrode studios' concerns about alienating ticket buyers with political films, which had been so important to the Production Code's project. Also, in the midst of the Depression, Hollywood artists and intellectuals looked for solutions to social and economic problems in communist, socialist, and fascist ideologies. Others actively opposed the rise of fascist and communist governments in Europe.

It was a time of political extremes in Hollywood, as indeed it was throughout the world. Charlie Chaplin and Orson Welles were some of the most outspoken figures on the Hollywood left, and they both gave antifascist speeches at rallies of the Popular Front, the loose amalgam of left-leaning groups. Excerpts of Chaplin's speeches made their way into his early sound films, and echoes of Welles's politics can be found in his first feature, *Citizen Kane* (1941), as well as other films he made in the 1940s.

More formally, the Hollywood Anti-Nazi League was founded in 1936 to oppose fascism. The League was a Communist Party front organization, founded at the instigation of the Communist Party USA (which was directly funded by the Soviet Communist Party), and card-carrying Communist screenwriter Donald Ogden Stewart chaired the league. But despite its party affiliation, the organization brought together the entire Hollywood spectrum: studio executives and writers, liberals and conservatives, Christians and Jews. Actor James Cagney, director John Ford, and Production Code Administration head Joseph Breen attended the organization's opening gala, which was cohosted by Stewart and Algonquin Roundtable doyenne Dorothy Parker.

The powerful group included studio heads Jack Warner and Carl Laemmle, and it championed labor unions and advocated for racial equality. The organization backed the Loyalists against the

Fascists in the Spanish Civil War, and it arranged large-scale protests when Mussolini's son Vittorio and Nazi filmmaker Leni Riefenstahl came to Hollywood. Mussolini's son was a producer trying to put together an international coproduction deal with Hollywood producer Hal Roach. Riefenstahl came to Los Angeles to meet with Walt Disney while attempting to arrange US distribution for her film about the 1936 Berlin Olympics, *Olympia* (1938).

After the Hitler-Stalin Pact of 1939 created a transitory alliance between the communist Soviet Union and fascist Germany, the Anti-Nazi League was forced to change its name to the Hollywood League for Democratic Action, and it lost its raison d'être. The Anti-Nazi League's heyday may have been brief, but it launched Hollywood into the global politics of the 1930s and prepared the way for active participation in the war. It would also open the door for criticism of Hollywood's politics in the coming decades.

Warner Bros. at war

When the United States finally entered the war, Hollywood sprang into action. Top movie stars lent their talent and celebrity in many ways. Clark Gable and Ronald Reagan voluntarily enlisted. Bob Hope and Shirley Temple signed up with the United Services Organization (USO) to perform for troops. James Cagney, Joan Crawford, Bette Davis, Melvyn Douglas, and John Garfield all spoke out against fascism. Some of the most successful studio directors, including Frank Capra, John Ford, John Huston, and William Wyler, joined the military to make documentary films.

Warner Bros., however, led the industry in its support for the war. The depression made for strange political alliances, and Jack and Harry Warner's devotion to FDR was certainly one of them. Like MGM head Louis B. Mayer, the Warner brothers had close ties to the Republican Party. But they bucked their party's line throughout the 1930s and 1940s not only to champion FDR's

6. Marlene Dietrich performs for US frontline soldiers. Entertaining troops was one of many ways that Hollywood supported the war effort during World War II.

New Deal and war plans but also to contribute to the lionization of FDR himself.

Warner Bros. eased into its role as the most patriotic studio. The Warner brothers began by insisting that studio employees donate to antifascist causes, and they cut off all studio ties with Germany in 1933, long before the other studios. Then, Warner Bros. began to express its American boosterism and antifascism in films. Starting in 1936, the studio made a number of short films celebrating American history. All of the studios still made shorts that played before features and served as a testing ground for new talent and ideas. In this case, Warner Bros. experimented by showing politically outspoken films to American audiences.

After some success, the studio brought its political agenda to feature films. Continuing to address contemporary politics through historical films, Warner Bros. released *The Life of Emile Zola* (1937), which alluded to the author's fight against anti-Semitism in nineteenth-century France. Then the studio tackled ripped-from-the-headlines events in a string of largely successful films endorsing wartime policies, explaining the war to American audiences, and, under military contracts, educating soldiers.

Warner Bros.' 1939 film *Confessions of a Nazi Spy* changed the playing field for the studios, and it opened the door for political films in Hollywood. It was the first major studio film to take on Nazism, and it had to win over the Production Code Administration and refashion many of the elements of the studio system for a world at war. As director, Warner Bros. chose Ukrainian-born Anatole Litvak, who had made films in Germany before fleeing the Nazis and ending up as a contract director on the Warner Bros. lot. Litvak's signature documentary-like style added authenticity to a politically brave film.

Confessions of a Nazi Spy stays as close to real events as possible, telling the story of a Nazi spy ring in the United States that was thwarted by the FBI. The film hits viewers over the head with its based-on-real-events message. It has a newsreel-style voice-of-god narration, and it uses the real names of the people depicted in the film to suggest that the studio is merely relating and not shaping its story.

But despite its reportage-like presentation, *Confessions of a Nazi Spy* still clearly fits the Hollywood mold. The documentary look is a thin veneer for a time-tested genre formula: the spy thriller narrative that concludes with a courtroom drama. And the cast is made up of familiar faces like those George Sanders and Francis Lederer. One of the studio's biggest stars, Edward G. Robinson, plays the heroic FBI agent, rebranding him as a hard-hitting force for justice, and preparing the ground for Warner Bros.' other stars

7. The first major studio film to take on the Nazis, *Confessions of a Nazi Spy* (Warner Bros., 1939) tells the true story of a spy ring in the United States. The film mixes documentary-style realism with popular stars such as George Sanders (*right*) and the familiar courtroom drama genre.

Bogart and Cagney to move from playing gangsters and lone wolves to taking on new roles as soldiers, resistance fighters, and company men.

Not only did the genre and star system have to fit a new mold, but the Production Code needed to be rethought for a changing political climate as well. *Confessions of a Nazi Spy* ignited internal disagreements within the Production Code Administration (PCA) office. The film represented a move into strongly nationalist politics. What if it offended American politicians or European audiences? What if the political climate changed quickly? The Third Reich took an active interest in policing Hollywood films, and it employed a full-time representative in Hollywood, Georg Gyssling, to ensure that Germany's interests were being served. Gyssling strenuously opposed *Confessions of a Nazi Spy*, but in the end PCA head Joseph Breen approved the film, saying that it honestly and fairly represented German politics and the German people.

It is likely that the PCA approved the film in part because the German market was all but closed off to Hollywood by 1939. The PCA helped films achieve fluid international circulation. If politics precluded distribution to a particular country, then the PCA seal was moot anyway. And, unsurprisingly, Germany and the Axis countries banned *Confessions of a Nazi Spy* after its release.

What is surprising is that the Warner Bros. gamble paid off. The film was a hit with audiences and critics, winning the best film award from the National Board of Review, which had become a critics' rather than a censors' organization by that point. *Confessions of a Nazi Spy* also opened the floodgates, leading a wave of political and especially anti-Nazi films in Hollywood. The next year Chaplin's *The Great Dictator* (United Artists, 1940) parodied Hitler; Frank Bozage's *The Mortal Storm* (MGM, 1940) explored the rise of Nazism in a small German town; and many films began to plug Nazis into stock villain roles. Deeper into the war, Hollywood produced a cycle of anti-Nazi films, including Edward Dmytryk's *Hitler's Children* (RKO, 1943) and Fritz Lang's *Ministry of Fear* (Paramount, 1944), that examined the details of Hitler's reign as stories came to light.

After the United States entered the war, Warner Bros. showed that Hollywood storytelling was perfectly prepared to humanize politics and imbue history with emotion. Warner Bros. started production on its big-budget patriotic diversion *Yankee Doodle Dandy* (1942) even before the bombing of Pearl Harbor. *Yankee Doodle Dandy* drew on the lessons of the studio's shorts to construct a biographical musical about Broadway legend George M. Cohan. It uses Cohan's career as a loose framework for stringing together the big patriotic song-and-dance numbers for which Cohan was famous: "You're a Grand Old Flag," "Over

There," and "Yankee Doodle Boy." The film whipped audiences into a frenzy around the American flag, which is featured prominently. And Warner Bros. gave the lead role to its top star, James Cagney, lending prominence to the film while also reflecting stars and stripes on Cagney, one of the studio's most precious commodities.

Yankee Doodle Dandy is related through a series of flashbacks illustrating stories that Cohan tells President Roosevelt. The audience watches Cohan from over FDR's shoulder, and we are presumably meant to identify with FDR as we celebrate America. It must have been jarring to have a sitting president impersonated in a major film, and *Yankee Doodle Dandy* opens with a self-conscious discussion of the pitfalls of depicting the current president. After the film's success, Warner Bros. continued to use the device in subsequent films, effectively linking the studio with the commander-in-chief. *Yankee Doodle Dandy* turned out to be a huge box office success, and it won three Oscars, including one for Cagney. It is still a fondly remembered favorite, just barely squeaking into the American Film Institute's list of the top 100 films at number 100.

But even a year or two after its release, audiences saw films like *Yankee Doodle Dandy* as simplistic propaganda. Years later, Warner Bros. mocked its own creation, as it did many of its other films, with a Bugs Bunny short. In *Yankee Doodle Bugs* (1954), Bugs Bunny recounts for his nephew Clyde how important rabbits were at pivotal moments in colonial American history. Obviously pro-rabbit propaganda, the stories mislead Clyde, who returns from his history exam wearing a dunce cap.

As the war dragged on, it took over more and more of Warner Bros.' resources. The studio made combat films like *Air Force* (1943) and *Objective, Burma!* (1945), which were designed to explain individual battles, missions, or theaters of war to audiences, an important task for a complex war fought on many fronts. These films were both grounded in facts and molded to fit studio genre formulas. Accuracy rarely trumped a dramatic story, and the British government was even moved to complain about how much *Objective, Burma!* centered on American troops instead of other Allied forces. The combat genre almost always had an allegorical dimension, in which squadrons were invariably made up of soldiers from diverse ethnic, class, and geographical backgrounds, who, like the country itself, came together in the service of democracy.

Warner Bros. also made films under contract for the military. Government contracting was a new business for Hollywood, and the major studio heads agreed to share the wealth. They formed the Research Council of the Academy of Motion Picture Arts and Sciences, which assigned government contracts to its members. In addition to the major studios, the Research Council included prominent independent producers Walter Wanger and Walt Disney (Disney would remain a minor, specialized studio until the 1970s).

One of Warner Bros.' contracts was for a series of educational cartoons about the character Private Snafu made between 1943 and 1945. Private Snafu (an acronym for "Situation normal, all fucked up") bumbles his way through military service, revealing the details of his orders to German spies and neglecting to take his malaria pills, among other costly mistakes. So that the severity of the issues was not lost in the humorous shorts, Private Snafu dies in several of the episodes. The soldiers lucky enough to be assigned to watch Private Snafu shorts were in for a treat. The cast and crew boasted some of the greatest talent in Hollywood, including Looney Tunes director Chuck Jones (a cult favorite today); the voice of Bugs Bunny and just about every major Warner Bros cartoon character, Mel Blank; and scripts by Theodore Geisel (aka Dr. Seuss).

The Private Snafu series took important lessons for military personnel and turned them into unforgettable confections embodied by a lovable character. It is exactly the kind of personal, emotional power that Hollywood could lend to otherwise dry wartime endeavors. Other standout shorts that achieved a similar effect include Warner Bros.' *You, John Jones!* (1943), in which James Cagney imagines what it would be like to be a Russian, Greek, or Chinese father whose family was being bombed by Axis powers. And in the War Department short *Autobiography of a "Jeep"* (1943), an anthropomorphized jeep narrates its own American dream tale: the military vehicle was born out of scientific ingenuity; it achieved success through grit and hard work; and it ended up in endless photo ops with celebrities and heads of state.

Making films about the vicissitudes of contemporary politics, however, could be controversial. In 1941, Germany broke its nonaggression pact and invaded the Soviet Union, forcing a delicate alliance between the United States and the Soviet Union. Warner Bros., as it had done before, jumped in first to address this new wartime development, adapting the memoir of former US ambassador to the Soviet Union Joseph E. Davies. *Mission to Moscow* (1943) looks like a natural successor to Warner Bros.' previous films, filtering recent political events through a biographical narrative and documentary-style presentation. The film was distributed with a prologue by Davies, who assures audiences that his only bias is that of a midwestern American educated in the public school system. He goes on to thank "those fine patriotic citizens, the Warner brothers," for telling his story. Helmed by *Yankee Doodle Dandy* director Michael Curtiz, *Mission to Moscow* reprises the impersonation of FDR, who, mostly off camera, instructs Davies to go to Germany and then the Soviet Union to learn all that he can about the Nazis and Soviets.

The film employs the documentary aesthetic that proved so effective in *Confessions of a Nazi Spy*, especially montage sequences of stock footage from Soviet archives and clips from the Nazi propaganda film *Triumph of the Will* (1935). Davies tours factories and meets with diplomats while his wife and daughter observe department stores and parties. Through didactic dialogue, they all come to realize that despite the goatees that every actor playing a Soviet man is made to wear, the United States and Soviet Union have more similarities than differences. In the final section of the film, Davies speaks to US politicians and Winston Churchill, making the pragmatic case for a US-Soviet wartime alliance.

Mission to Moscow was less financially and critically successful than many of Warner Bros.' other wartime films, but it did kick off a cycle of films about Russia released over the next two years: *The Boy from Stalingrad* (Columbia, 1943), *The North Star* (RKO, 1943), *Three Russian Girls* (United Artists, 1943), *Song of Russia* (MGM, 1944), and *Counter-Attack* (Columbia, 1945). These were far from revolutionary films, but after the war they would come under close scrutiny during investigations into potential communist infiltration of Hollywood. Like most of the films made by Hollywood during the war, the Russian cycle brought a human dimension to the geopolitics of World War II. Hollywood's wartime film production brought European and Asian cultures to life for movie audiences, and they explained in moral terms what Americans were fighting for.

Wartime government agencies

The Hollywood studios did not promote the war unchaperoned. Starting in the 1930s, the Production Code had proven to be a valuable tool for standardizing movie narratives and managing films' moral and political messages. Making movies for wartime required even more risk and complications. Some overseas markets closed, and others became more important. Public opinion about the war shifted quickly, and getting accurate military information out was important. For all of these reasons, plus the Department of Justice's and Selective Service's efforts to help the film industry, Hollywood studios worked willingly with a range of government agencies that oversaw wartime production and distribution.

The Office of Censorship cleared films for import and export, and its staff decided whether films had the potential to be valuable to the enemy. Did they jeopardize national security, show sensitive military installations, or disparage the US military? The office also evaluated depictions of Americans and allies that were sent abroad. The PCA continued to insure that films were not offensive to political parties or national governments, but the Office of Censorship often overrode the PCA, blocking films that the PCA approved.

In 1942, the Office of Censorship convinced Republic Pictures to shelve *Fu Manchu Strikes Back*, because of its offensive Chinese stereotypes. And in an ironic twist, Frank Capra's frequent screenwriter Robert Riskin found himself working for the Office of Censorship and banning a film for export that he had written, *Meet John Doe* (1941), presumably because it shows Americans ready to embrace socialism and susceptible to crypto-fascist manipulation.

The Office of War Information (OWI) had the broadest mandate to oversee the American film industry. The OWI presided over all domestic and exported US media, including Hollywood, which reported to the OWI's Bureau of Motion Pictures. Like the PCA, the OWI reviewed ideas, scripts, and rough cuts of films. The OWI, however, was more proactive than the PCA. The OWI not only commented on filmmakers' work; its staff often fed filmmakers war details, script ideas, and even prepared speeches that they hoped would be included in films. The OWI produced a weekly newsreel of its own, but its primary job was to monitor existing film companies. In 1942 the Bureau of Motion Pictures issued *The Government Informational Manual for the Motion Picture Industry*, which expanded on many of the political directives already in the Production Code. The manual cautioned against expressing racism, religious intolerance, and class prejudice, warning that such sentiments "are manifestations of fascism and should be exposed as such." The OWI wanted to ensure that the United States appeared to be a tolerant democratic society.

The OWI staff turned out to be early fans of the cult classic *Casablanca* (1942). Michael Curtiz directed *Casablanca* for Warner Bros. in between *Yankee Doodle Dandy* and *Mission to Moscow*, and it seemed to capture the country's mood in a more offhanded way than the two calculated efforts that bookended it. *Casablanca* is the story of American expatriate cafe owner, Rick (Humphrey Bogart), who has to decide whether to help a French resistance fighter, Victor Laszlo (Paul Henreid), escape to America. As an added complication, Rick is in love with Laszlo's wife, Ilsa (Ingrid Bergman), and, moreover, like America itself, Rick is trying to remain neutral even as Nazis, French soldiers, embattled North Africans, and European refugees pass through his cafe. But Rick is continually drawn into political disputes, because he cares about the people involved. It may be the perfect expression of Hollywood's personalization of the war.

The OWI viewed *Casablanca* on October 26, 1942, just before the British invasion of North Africa, and the OWI notes praised the film for showing that individual sentiments, like Rick's love for Ilsa, needed to be subordinated to fight against fascism. The OWI also liked that the film depicts America as a haven for the dispossessed: everyone in Rick's cafe is in search of exit visas to America, the land of freedom. Finally, the OWI praised Rick's brief mention of his own history fighting against fascism in Spain and France. Rick's and America's reasons for getting involved in the war did not start with Pearl Harbor but stem from a long history of fighting for democracy on a global scale. The perceptive film viewers at the OWI recognized the allegorical implications of *Casablanca*, as would most 1940s audiences.

The OWI's purview stopped at the border of Latin America, which belonged to Rockefeller family scion Nelson Rockefeller's Office of the Coordinator of Inter-American Affairs (CIAA). Rockefeller had his fingers in many pies—business, politics, culture—and he would go on to have a long political career as governor of New York and vice president of the United States. During World War II Latin America became an important export market for Hollywood and an equally important political battleground for the US government discouraging fascist and communist infiltration. With European distribution cut off, Hollywood ramped up production of films for export to Latin America, and Rockefeller was eager to help. In addition to overseeing content like the OWI did, Rockefeller's agency also offered insurance for films made in or for Latin America. Orson Welles traveled to Brazil to make a film under the CIAA terms. But the project fell apart, like so many of Welles's other projects, and eventually some of his footage was released a half century later as *It's All True* (1993).

Rockefeller's most dramatic intervention was made on behalf of the Disney studio. When Walt Disney failed to settle a strike with his animators, Rockefeller stepped in as CIAA head. Rockefeller sent Disney on a diplomatic tour of Latin America, where he showed films and talked to audiences. While Disney was away, a federal mediator negotiated terms for the end of the strike. Once the animators were back in the studio, they set to work making films for Latin American audiences, including *Saludos Amigos* (1942) and *The Three Caballeros* (1944).

These wartime cultural agencies were controversial from the time of their inception. Was their mandate to insure that media disseminated accurate information about the war, or did they constitute an American propaganda ministry? During the House of Representatives' budget hearings of 1943, Republican members of Congress worried that FDR had created his own personal propaganda agency, which had the potential to be invaluable during future elections. The House cut funding to OWI completely. The Senate agreed to close the OWI's domestic branch and the Motion Picture Bureau, but it restored some funding to the overseas branches, which countered enemy propaganda through the end of the war. After the war, the State Department took over some elements of the wartime agencies, and the 1948 Smith-Mundt Act made it illegal for the US government to propagandize its own citizens.

Chapter 5
The blacklist and the Cold War

Hollywood's foray into politics during World War II had major repercussions in the postwar period. It led to standoffs with conservative factions in Congress, fractured the Hollywood community, and prompted the studios to take extreme actions to win back American moviegoers.

HUAC in Hollywood

Even before the United States entered the war, anti–New Deal Republicans in Congress attacked the film studios—singling out Warner Bros.—for pushing the country toward military intervention. After the war, the House Committee on Un-American Activities, or HUAC, became a standing Congressional committee. Opportunistic members of Congress rode a wave of anticommunism and renewed the offensive against Hollywood. The committee hearings were media spectacles, creating front-page headlines and, in the 1950s, a television media circus as well.

Outspoken anticommunist Senator Joseph McCarthy is often mistakenly thought to have been a member of HUAC, but he had his own Senate committee that investigated alleged communist infiltration of the government. Although McCarthy did not participate in the Hollywood hearings, the vicious personal attacks for political gain that came to be called McCarthyism destroyed many promising Hollywood careers, and it boosted the careers of politicians, including future presidents Richard Nixon and Ronald Reagan.

At first, HUAC went after the activities of the Anti-Nazi League and looked for communist messages in *Mission to Moscow* and other films from the Soviet cycle. But the committee members soon learned that taking on major party donors like the Hollywood moguls was politically messy, and locating hidden communist messages in films was not a clear-cut task.

The committee quickly turned to questioning well-known actors and directors, whose celebrity attracted public interest to their cause. During the hearings, writers, directors, actors, and producers took the stand, forever changing their personal and professional lives. It was a period of soul searching, strained friendships, and often dire circumstances. More than a half century later, HUAC testimony continues to reverberate in the film industry and beyond.

One of the first Hollywood representatives to talk to HUAC was Eric Johnston. Johnston assumed the leadership of the MPPDA— by then renamed the Motion Picture Association of America— from Will Hays. Testifying before HUAC, Johnston read a reasonable statement, claiming that there were in fact some communists in Hollywood and that it was their right to hold radical political views as long as they did not advocate the overthrow of the US government. Johnston may have been both technically and morally right. There were communists in Hollywood (three hundred by one count), and the First Amendment gave them the right to voice politically unpopular views. But as Johnston would later learn, these were extreme times, and even basic constitutional rights were in limbo.

HUAC continued to call witnesses from all sides of the issue. On the government's side were "friendly" witnesses, who corroborated

HUAC's assertions that communists lurked in the movie industry. Friendly witnesses were largely drawn from the ranks of a Hollywood group called the Motion Picture Alliance for the Preservation of American Ideals. The organization included conservative anticommunist actors and directors Gary Cooper, Cecil B. DeMille, Clark Gable, Leo McCary, Adolphe Menjou, Ronald Reagan, Ginger Rogers, Barbara Stanwyck, King Vidor, and John Wayne.

Of the friendly witnesses only one, Ayn Rand, affirmed that Hollywood films harbored procommunist messages. Rand was born Alisa Rosenbaum in Russia and immigrated to the United States with her family. She appeared as an extra in Cecil B. DeMille's *King of Kings* (1927) and worked as a screenwriter in Hollywood before achieving bestseller success as a novelist and free market evangelist.

On the stand, Rand wore a gold pin shaped like a dollar sign, just in case her capitalist allegiances were in doubt. And she explained to the committee that MGM's 1944 *Song of Russia* promoted communism simply by showing happy Soviet citizens. When Representative John McDowell asked her, jokingly, "Doesn't anybody smile in Russia anymore?" Rand answered humorlessly, "Well, if you ask me literally, pretty much no."

Rand had hoped to give more extensive testimony, showing that procommunist messages could also be found in William Wyler's popular postwar drama about American soldiers returning home, *The Best Years of Our Lives* (1946), in addition to films explicitly about Russia. But the committee decided not to take on a commercially successful film and limited her to talking about *Song of Russia*.

If HUAC refused to give Rand the megaphone, she took it herself. In response, Rand wrote a pamphlet called *Screen Guide for Americans*, which was published by the Motion Picture Alliance for the Preservation of American Ideals and reprinted on the front page of the *New York Times* arts section. The pamphlet taught filmgoers how to identify procommunist messages in films, and it showed lefty screenwriters how to keep their films red, white, and blue.

Other friendly witnesses all agreed that no communist propaganda had yet appeared in Hollywood films, although they worried about the possibility. HUAC questioned Jack Warner about *Mission to Moscow* more than once. If any Hollywood film was pro-Soviet, it was *Mission to Moscow*, with its unquestioning defense of Soviet premier Joseph Stalin, who personally endorsed the film after its release.

Jack Warner had different explanations for the movie on different occasions. First he blamed it on Washington but then recanted the position that the government had been involved in the film's production. Later, Warner explained that *Mission to Moscow* had been made to have a particular effect at a particular moment in the war just as US ships carried food and arms to Russia, an American ally at the time, but might not have aided the Soviet Union later. For the most part, HUAC went easy on Jack Warner, who was instrumental in encouraging the committee and the FBI to investigate Hollywood.

When identifying communist propaganda in films proved complicated, HUAC switched its focus to hunting communists in the industry, and the committee quickly learned to go after the biggest names it could find. When HUAC subpoenaed American icon Walt Disney as a friendly witness, he was still stinging from his animators' strike. Before the committee, Disney swiftly brushed aside any suggestion that his studio's films could be tinged with communism, claiming that Russia had sent back Disney cartoons, because "they didn't suit their purposes."

Instead, Disney used the public forum to tell the members of Congress how one malcontent in his studio, Herbert K. Sorrell, who Disney thought was probably a communist, stirred up all of the trouble that led to his animators' strike. Disney told a cautionary tale of Sorrell threatening his business and upsetting his employees, who were now, he was glad to say, back to being "100 percent American." It was a well-dramatized parable about how even a single communist could infiltrate and destroy the most American of institutions—exactly what one would expect from a Disney story. Ironically, when Soviet filmmaker Sergei Eisenstein visited Disney's studio in 1941, he praised it as a perfect workers' collective, with everyone laboring toward the same goal.

Ronald Reagan, then head of the Screen Actors Guild, offered testimony that perfectly echoed Disney's. Even before testifying, Reagan had been an active informant for the FBI, alerting the agency to potential communists in the industry. On the stand, Reagan claimed that a "disruptive element"—he avoided the word communist—had infiltrated the guild and attempted to use unscrupulous tactics to convert other members. Reagan inferred that as much as 10 percent of the guild had such disruptive leanings. Later, Reagan insisted that all guild members take an oath expressing their loyalty to the United States, as did many other businesses at the time. Cecil B. DeMille lobbied for the Directors Guild to adopt a loyalty oath, but his motion failed, and it provoked lifelong feuds. Although Reagan worried about the presence of communists, he assured HUAC that there would never be any left-wing propaganda in Hollywood films.

Conservative Hollywood leaders like Warner, Disney, and Reagan were valuable, but reformed communists were the most prized friendly witnesses. When suspected communists were called before the committee they had to answer two questions. First they were asked, "Are you now or have you ever been a member of the Communist Party?" It was not enough to admit membership, however. If a witness admitted Communist Party affiliation, he or she also had to name other members ("name names"). These were often names of people already known to be involved with the party, but it could still be very troubling to point a finger at a friend and colleague. Some of the famous actors and directors who admitted party affiliation and named names of other communists include actors Lee J. Cobb and Sterling Hayden (who deeply regretted his decision), director Edward Dmytryk, and writer Clifford Odets.

HUAC questioned some of the biggest names in Hollywood, but the committee ran into a public relations disaster when it subpoenaed Lucille Ball, the star of the top-rated television show *I Love Lucy* (1951–1960). Just months before her HUAC testimony, the episode of *I Love Lucy* in which Lucy gives birth drew a larger audience than President Eisenhower's inauguration the following week. If the committee drove everyone's favorite program off the air, it would certainly have made HUAC unpopular. Ball had not been a member of the Communist Party, but, following the lead of her socialist grandfather, in 1936 she filed a form indicating that she intended to register to vote as a communist.

Even this flimsy leftist history was enough to destroy an actor in the anxious climate of the 1950s. But Lucy was special, and HUAC arranged for her to give private testimony in Los Angeles, in which she told her story and named some already well-known communists. When *I Love Lucy* was filmed later the same day (the show was filmed rather than broadcast live like most others), Ball's costar and husband Desi Arnaz told the studio audience, "The only thing red about [Lucy] is her hair, and even that is not legitimately red." In a brilliant ploy, Arnaz gave the quote to reporters, and he changed the conversation from politics to hair dye. And both HUAC and Lucille Ball retained their popularity.

The most outspoken friendly witness—and still the most controversial—was Elia Kazan. Kazan had been a member of the Communist Party for two years in the 1930s, and he had a brilliant career as a left-leaning theater and film director. When called to testify before HUAC, Kazan did more than admit to his past party membership and identify eight of his former colleagues in the Group Theater as communists; Kazan also launched a campaign to justify his actions. At his own expense, he placed an ad in the *New York Times*, claiming that it was every American's duty to share information they might have about the "dangerous and alien conspiracy" afoot.

Kazan then went on to make *On the Waterfront* (1954), in which Marlon Brando plays a dockworker who informs on his corrupt friends and relatives. The powerful film makes the ethical case for informing, and it responds to *The Crucible* (1953), a play written by Kazan's old friend and collaborator Arthur Miller. Miller's allegorical play about the Salem witch trials explores how mobs (like those that supported HUAC) can distort reality and be led to a collective evil that no one person might be capable of on their own. In contrast, *On the Waterfront* celebrates whistleblowers who tell the truth for the benefit of society even when it may hurt them personally.

8. In this scene from HUAC friendly witness Elia Kazan's *On the Waterfront* (Columbia Pictures, 1954), Marlon Brando makes the case for informing.

Of course Kazan benefited from his testimony. He went on to create an impressive body of films after appearing before HUAC, but he did it by supporting a movement that destroyed the careers of his friends and colleagues. And both Kazan's actions and the HUAC investigations remain an open wound in Hollywood. When the Academy of Motion Picture Arts and Sciences awarded Kazan an honorary Oscar in 1999, half of the audience clapped while the other half sat on their hands.

The Hollywood Ten and the blacklist

Many witnesses were not friendly, and the members of the Hollywood community who took the other route, who stood up for their First Amendment rights or who refused to incriminate others, lost the opportunity to work in the film industry; they were blacklisted. For the most part, they did not go on to make more films, and their legacy is their resistance to an unjust crusade rather than a long filmography.

The first group of unfriendly witnesses is known as the Hollywood Ten. In 1947, HUAC called before the committee eleven witnesses who indicated that they would refuse to answer questions. When playwright Bertolt Brecht returned to his native Germany, ten unfriendly witnesses were left: Alvah Bessie, Herbert J. Biberman, Lester Cole, Edward Dmytryk, Ring Lardner Jr., John Howard Lawson, Albert Maltz, Samuel Ornitz, Adrian Scott, and Dalton Trumbo. This group revealed the anti-Semitic zeal that drove Mississippi congressman John Rankin and other HUAC members. Six of the Hollywood Ten were Jewish, and three of the remaining four had recently completed *Crossfire* (1947), a cinematic condemnation of anti-Semitism. Personal prejudice mixed with political anxieties to make a potent combination.

Progressive Hollywood celebrities rallied to the defense of the Ten. John Huston, William Wyler, Danny Kaye, Lauren Bacall, Humphrey Bogart, and others formed the Committee for the First

Amendment. They flew to Washington and marched to protect the constitutional rights of the Ten. But when the witnesses spoke before HUAC, they did more than just refuse to answer questions; they were belligerent and alienated some of their most ardent defenders. HUAC found them to be in contempt of Congress, and studio leadership quickly distanced themselves from the Ten.

Executives met with Eric Johnston at the Waldorf-Astoria Hotel in New York and released what became known as the Waldorf Statement. The new statement contradicted Johnston's earlier defense of freedom of speech and thought. It said that the studios would "not knowingly hire a communist," and with that the blacklist began, banning anyone suspected of subversive affiliations from working in Hollywood. It gave the studios broad latitude to dismiss employees regardless of contracts or collective agreements with talent guilds. Many moguls, like Jack Warner, truly feared communist infiltration. But the anticommunist hysteria also increased the studios' power over their employees.

Two members of the Ten, John Howard Lawson and Dalton Trumbo, appealed their contempt conviction in court, convinced that the Supreme Court would have to uphold their constitutional rights. But the US District Court of Appeals in Washington, DC, upheld the contempt charge. The Lawson-Trumbo decision referenced the high stakes of the political atmosphere, as if that somehow put the Constitution on hiatus. "No one can doubt in these chaotic times," the decision read, "that the destiny of all nations hangs in the balance in the current ideological struggle between communist-thinking and democratic-thinking peoples of the world." It went on, like the 1915 Mutual decision had, to give Hollywood special status as an opinion maker. The court described movies as "a potent medium of propaganda," and the decision warned that Hollywood "plays a critically prominent role in the molding of public opinion." Hollywood filmmakers' free speech rights were once again deferred. The Supreme Court, newly stacked with conservative justices, declined to hear the case, and the members of the Hollywood Ten each served six months to a year in prison.

With the Supreme Court's tacit endorsement, the blacklist was in full force, and it destroyed the careers of a generation of talented writers, actors, directors, and producers. Blacklisted director Joseph Losey moved to England, and director Jules Dassin moved to France. They were the lucky ones who found work outside of Hollywood. Screenwriter Lester Cole worked in a warehouse, and screenwriter Sidney Buchman operated a parking garage. Other stories ended in tragedy. Television star Philip Loeb committed suicide after being blacklisted, and rising star John Garfield died of a heart attack brought on in part by the stress of being blacklisted.

The blacklist was not a published list of names. Hollywood trade papers tried to compile lists of communists, and a 1950 book, *Red Channels*, attempted to identify communists in the broadcast industry. Many people named in these lists were called before HUAC and stopped working. But the blacklist was more insidious. Studios distanced themselves from writers, actors, and directors based on reputations. Appearing as an unfriendly witness before HUAC would certainly destroy someone's reputation. But whispers about connections and affiliations were also enough to damage careers.

Some writers were able to continue working through fronts, nonblacklisted writers who sold scripts for them. Fronts took a big risk associating with blacklisted writers, and the ruse could be difficult to keep up in the small company town of Los Angeles. Martin Ritt's 1976 film *The Front*, starring Woody Allen, perfectly dramatized both the appeal and dangers of the situation. The front in the film, played by Allen, enjoys fame, money, and success on the work of the blacklistees until coming under HUAC scrutiny himself.

One of the most successful writers to use fronts and pseudonyms was Hollywood Ten member Dalton Trumbo. Trumbo had been a highly regarded writer before the blacklist. His HUAC defiance had serious ramifications, and he spent time in jail, ran out of money, and moved to Mexico at one point. But Trumbo was dedicated to his craft. He kept writing, and he sold scripts through many fronts, accepting far less in payment than he would have using his own name and selling to producers directly.

Eventually, Trumbo's covert writing became an open secret. At the 1956 Academy Awards, the screenwriting Oscar went to Robert Rich for *The Brave One*. When no one came to the stage to accept the award, everyone in the industry seemed to know that Trumbo was the real author. Trumbo even suggested as much in a television interview the next day. Four years later, and thirteen years after his HUAC testimony, Trumbo became the first blacklisted writer to receive screen credit. His name appeared in the credits of two films that year, *Spartacus* and *Exodus*. Dalton Trumbo broke the Hollywood blacklist, but the blacklist itself never officially ended. Many blacklisted writers, actors, and directors never worked in the industry again.

Cold War films

In the 1950s, Hollywood fought communism onscreen and off. Shortly after the MPAA issued the Waldorf Statement in 1947, all of the studios set to work producing explicitly anticommunist films. These were rarely big-budget, star-studded movies, but they served a number of political and commercial ends. They demonstrated the studios' commitment to fighting communism just as Hollywood was coming under attack as a haven for left-leaning artists. The anticommunist cycle also connected with American Cold War anxieties, and the films in the cycle were generally successful at the box office and occasionally on the awards circuit.

Between 1942 and 1953, Hollywood released dozens of film about the "red menace" of communism, including William Wellman's

Iron Curtain (1948); *The Red Menace* (1949); *The Red Danube* (1949); *Conspirator* (1949), starring Elizabeth Taylor and Robert Taylor; *My Son John* (1952), directed by outspoken Hollywood conservative Leo McCary; *Red Snow* (1952); and *The Steel Fist* (1952). By 1953, director Samuel Fuller's noir crime film *Pickup on South Street* showed, communist spies had replaced gangsters as generic Hollywood villains.

Other films took up Cold War themes and the blacklist more metaphorically. *Force of Evil* (1948), directed by Abraham Polonsky and starring John Garfield shortly before they were blacklisted, used number running as a metaphor for capitalism. The opening shot of Wall Street solidified the metaphor. The film presents a dark view of a world in which the only choices are between different corrupt institutions. The Production Code Administration—always worried about strong political films—insisted that the film have a moral center, which is provided ambiguously through a voice-over. The PCA also rejected the screenplay's framing device of telling the story through witness-stand flashbacks, because in 1948 that would have brought HUAC too clearly to mind for audiences, just as the filmmakers had intended.

A cycle of westerns, always a highly allegorical genre, took up the politics of informing and mob rule, although today it is possible to watch many of these films without noticing any reference to the blacklist at all. In Nicholas Ray's *Johnny Guitar* (1954) a posse forces an outlaw to identify a tavern owner, played by Joan Crawford, as a conspirator, even though most of the townspeople know she is innocent.

The Gary Cooper western *High Noon* (1952) also addressed Hollywood's response to HUAC. If there were political debates on the set of *High Noon*, they must have been heated. Cooper had been a friendly witness before HUAC and was a founder of the Motion Picture Alliance for the Preservation of American Ideals.

Other actors in the film, Lloyd Bridges and Howard Chamberlain, were later blacklisted. Screenwriter Carl Forman was also slated to be blacklisted, but apparently Gary Cooper successfully fought to keep him employed by the studio until after the film was over. Producer Stanley Kramer was an outspoken liberal, yet he chose to feature a theme song by reactionary Republican Tex Ritter.

With the full political spectrum represented both in front of and behind the camera, one might expect *High Noon* to be a film with mixed messages, and indeed it is an allegory open to multiple readings. In the film, Cooper plays the lone marshal of a western town, trying to protect it from three villains. The key line of the film comes when Cooper enters the church and asks for help, only to be met with excuses from everyone in the community. In a 1950s western, a marshal asking for help was a major genre twist, a sign of weakness in the lone hero. The most common reading of the film, and the one that prevailed at the time, is that Cooper represents a subpoenaed witness left to fend for himself against the HUAC villains. But in another interpretation, the villains could stand in for communists, with Cooper as the defender of American values. The meaning may have been up for debate, but the film was clearly seen as a Cold War allegory, and John Wayne called it the "most un-American movie" he had ever seen. Wayne responded by making *Big Jim McLain* (1952), which glamorized HUAC investigators.

Westerns had always been canvases for ritually working through American transformations. In the 1950s, science fiction films also seemed to absorb the anticommunist anxieties of the period, with popular cycles of alien invasion films and giant insect infestations. Director Don Siegel's *Invasion of the Body Snatchers* (1956) quintessentially exploited one of the most frightening (to their opponents) aspects of communists: they look like everyone else. Communists are only different on the inside, and even your neighbor or boss or child could be a communist. *Invasion of the Body Snatchers* plays on this fear, and in the film aliens grow pod people to replace townspeople with identical doubles who take orders from the aliens.

In the late 1950s and early 1960s, anticommunist fears became the subject of parody. In the musical *Silk Stockings* (1957), Fred Astaire woos Soviet functionary Cyd Charisse, and everyone succumbs to the excesses of Parisian nightlife. In Stanley Kubrick's *Dr. Strangelove* (1964), paranoid general Jack D. Ripper, played by former reluctant friendly witness Sterling Hayden, worries about communists neutralizing his virility though fluoridation. And Cold War cultural diplomacy reached the level of high farce in Billy Wilder's *One, Two, Three* (1961), in which James Cagney graduated from playing 1930s gangsters and World War II soldiers to starring as a Coca-Cola executive–diplomat in Cold War West Berlin.

During this period, Charlie Chaplin shed his Little Tramp character and became a politically engaged filmmaker for the sound era, making some of his funniest and most trenchant films. He also had the last word in Hollywood's standoff with HUAC. In 1940, *The Great Dictator* lampooned Hitler as a setup for a humanistic call for peace delivered at the film's climax. In *Monsieur Verdoux* (1947), Chaplin plays a Bluebeard character, serially marrying and murdering women across Europe. Just when he seems morally reprehensible, Verdoux turns the tables, explaining that, compared to the mass murderers leading the world's nations, his killing spree makes him an amateur.

In his penultimate film, *A King in New York* (1957), Chaplin finally gets to act out the HUAC testimony that he avoided in real life. HUAC subpoenaed Chaplin several times, but he never took the stand. Chaplin did, however, have continued friction with the FBI, and when promoting his film *Limelight* abroad in 1952, the US Immigration and Naturalization Service insisted that Chaplin be interviewed before returning to the United States. Chaplin refused the interview and stayed out of the country for two decades.

In *A King in New York*, Chaplin plays a deposed monarch living in New York. The king is mistakenly suspected of being a communist, because of his associations, and he is summoned to appear before HUAC. On the way to the committee room, Chaplin gets his finger caught in a hose, which is still attached to him as he raises his hand to take the oath before the committee. When someone connects the other end of the hose to a water faucet, Chaplin inadvertently drenches the committee members, and his view of HUAC becomes clear: they are all wet.

Chapter 6
The New Hollywood

Starting immediately after World War II, the Hollywood studio system entered a period of major transformation, and by the late 1960s a New Hollywood emerged. Some of the influences that remade Hollywood include Americans' postwar flight to the suburbs, the rise of the 1960s counterculture, the resolution of the ongoing antitrust case against the studios, the popularity of foreign films in the United States, and the passing away of the original studio moguls to usher in a new wave of industry leaders. With pressure from all sides, the factory-like studios of Hollywood's Golden Age morphed into multimedia conglomerates focused at first on making personal films and later on making auteur-driven blockbusters.

Television

One of the biggest changes to have an impact on Hollywood starting in the 1950s was the widespread adoption of television. Like so many other new technologies, television appeared as a threat to Hollywood before it was recognized as a vital addition to the studio system. Although new media are often feared by Hollywood leaders, they rarely replace old media; new and old media redefine each other.

Starting in the 1910s, for example, going to the movies meant an evening or afternoon of entertainment: a cartoon, a newsreel, a serial, a B movie, and then a big-budget feature. After the advent of television, every item on the film program except the feature film migrated to the small screen. With free news and serials in the living room and a suburban leisure culture on the rise, movie attendance dropped precipitously. At its peak in 1946, Hollywood sold ninety-eight million tickets a week. By 1962 attendance was a quarter of the 1946 height.

The smaller studios like Monogram and Republic, sometimes known as "Poverty Row" studios, immediately saw the value of television. They sold their film libraries to the networks in the early 1950s and went into the made-for-television movie business. But the larger studios refused to license their film libraries, and they put their energy into creating bigger theatrical spectacles that could lure suburbanites off of their sofas and away from their backyards.

In the 1940s, the great French critic André Bazin looked at black and white, two-dimensional, square-framed film and claimed that "cinema has not yet been invented." For Bazin, film would only realize its potential when it imitated our perception of reality more completely, as color, widescreen, and 3-D processes could. As so often happens, it took competition, in this case from television, to bring new technologies to the screen. And in the 1950s, Hollywood set out on a mission to one-up television and approach the ideal perceptual experience Bazin termed "total cinema."

Most of these experiments in improving the theatrical experience were short-lived. There had been promising color film processes as early as the 1910s, for example, but Hollywood used color modestly. At the beginning of the 1950s, only 20 percent of studio films were released in color. Spurred by television, that number rose to 50 percent by the middle of the decade, only to return to below 20 percent once it became clear that television would be a new market for films rather than competition. It was only in the mid-1960s when color televisions created a sufficient aftermarket that studios began to convert completely to color.

Widescreen and 3-D also promised to create a theatrical film experience that would coax movie patrons away from their television sets. Like color, the history of widescreen and 3-D experimentation stretches far back in film history and progressed in fits and starts. For a brief moment in 1952 and 1953 the studios invested heavily in new technological experiments, only to discard 3-D altogether and scale back widescreen plans considerably.

Before the 1950s, films were generally shot in a narrow rectangular format, using the standard film aspect ratio of 1.375 (horizontal) to 1 (vertical), also known as Academy ratio. When televisions were first produced, they used an aspect ratio of 1.33 to 1, just slightly narrower than film. In response, Hollywood toyed with a number of widescreen formats. Cinerama, the boldest entry in the field, used three cameras, three projectors, and a curved screen to create an image that exceeded the range of viewers' peripheral vision. Premiering in 1952, Cinerama returned filmgoers to the fairground with travelogues and films that resembled amusement park rides. In *This Is Cinerama* (1952), a film made to showcase the new format, cameras were placed on boats, planes, and roller-coasters. Audiences were enveloped by the image and immersed in the action.

Some studios continued to make a few Cinerama films each year until 1962. But almost as soon as Cinerama premiered, Hollywood adopted a more moderate widescreen alternative. Rather than refitting every theater with new screens and multiple projectors, the studios and exhibitors decided to use a widescreen format called CinemaScope. CinemaScope required only the use of new lenses in cameras and projectors. CinemaScope lenses compress a wide rectangular image onto a strip of 35mm film, only to expand it again when it is projected. This process, known as anamorphosis, is the visual equivalent of compressing a toy spring snake in a jar and watching it expand after the cap is removed.

The CinemaScope image is still more than double the width of the television image, with an aspect ratio of 2.35 to 1 (or more, depending on the sound system used). Twentieth Century Fox blazed the CinemaScope trail with three films in 1953, *The Robe*, *How to Marry a Millionaire*, and *Beneath the 12-Mile Reef*, and most other studios quickly followed. CinemaScope delivered a big theatrical experience that could not be rivaled by television's small, square box.

Making outsized films was the goal, but eventually, when studios wanted their films adapted to television, widescreen formats posed problems. The films either had to be "letterboxed," shrunk down to fit across the screen, leaving empty black bars above and below, or they had to be "panned and scanned," showing only a part of each shot.

The theatrical version of *Ghostbusters* (1984), for example, features four members of the ghostbuster team, but in the panned and scanned version made for television, Ernie, the African American ghostbuster, gets very little screen time, since it was difficult to fit all four actors in the narrower frame. Squeezing widescreen films onto small screens became a problem for cell phone users too. Early versions of the iPhone, for example, had aspect ratios of 1.5 to 1, which is adequate for early television and pre-1953 movies. But even the iPhone 5 (released in 2012), with a 1.78 to 1 aspect ratio, fell short of CinemaScope.

Stereoscopic (3-D) film has had many short-lived vogues, but the period from 1952 to 1954 has a special place in the history of 3-D. A cycle of horror and science fiction 3-D films generated widespread enthusiasm both within the industry and among the public. After United Artists distributed the 3-D color adventure film *Bwana Devil* (1952), many studios made moderately budgeted 3-D films, including Columbia's *Man in the Dark* and Warner Bros.' *House of Wax* (both 1953). The latter film featured Vincent Price, who would become a cult horror film star, and it was one of the first films to have a stereophonic soundtrack (stereo sound was another means used to lure audiences away from their televisions, although only the top theaters were equipped stereo sound systems). Like the hula hoop, 3-D became an emblematic 1950s fad, widely memorialized with photos of large movie theaters full of patrons wearing the red-and-blue-tinted 3-D glasses used by some systems.

By the end of 1953, however, it was already clear that films being shot with 3-D cameras, like Alfred Hitchcock's *Dial M for Murder*, would be released in 2-D. Many theories have been proposed to account for 3-D's repeated failure to become an industry standard. The 3-D format may be better suited to avant-garde experimentation than to mainstream entertainment. Producing 3-D films may never become affordable for most filmmakers. Audiences may never adjust to watching 3-D images through uncomfortable eyewear. Another explanation for 3-D's continual rise and fall, however, is that the format has perpetually been used as a short-term means of competing with new small-screen technologies, first television and later home video and cell phones. Hollywood has consistently lost interest in 3-D as soon as the industry learned to stop worrying about, and start loving, new technologies.

As they had with the introduction of sound, Hollywood had a two-pronged approach to television, simultaneously resisting and incorporating the new medium. While the studios made bigger and more spectacular films, they also prepared to sell films to television. First, the studios had to negotiate with the actors, writers, and others who worked on the films, since television rights were not part of the initial contracts. Once a payment structure was in place for airing films on television, the studios had to negotiate the sale of their extensive libraries. In 1955 RKO sold its library for $15 million, and then Warner Bros. sold its library for $21 million, prices that would have been much higher a few years later. The same year, NBC and Twentieth Century Fox launched *Saturday Night at the Movies*, to showcase films on television.

Many of the studios also began to make shows exclusively for television. The talent agency Music Corporation of America (MCA) ran the largest television production company, Revue, and also acquired Universal Studios. Columbia Pictures entered the television production business as early as 1949, making the popular show *Father Knows Best*. In 1954 Disney and ABC struck a deal; ABC invested in Disney's theme park scheme, and Disney began to produce a weekly television series called *Disneyland*, which contained some original content and also promoted Disney films and amusement park. Over the next few years, Disney produced highly popular shows, including *The Mickey Mouse Club* and *Zorro*.

MGM, Twentieth Century Fox, and Warner Bros. all began producing TV shows too, which like Disney's both offered new content and promoted their films. By 1965, 70 percent of television programming came from Hollywood, and synergies between movies and television became part of the calculus for producing new projects. If television started out as a threat to Hollywood, by the mid-1960s it was just another cog in the studio system's machine.

Hollywood auteurs

Alongside technological developments, Hollywood had to adapt to two Supreme Court decisions that dramatically altered the structure of the studio system. First, the Department of Justice resumed the antitrust case it had been building for decades, and the investigation culminated in the 1948 Paramount decision, in which the court found Hollywood to be acting anticompetitively. Before the decision, the film industry was vertically integrated, and its block booking practices made it difficult for independent producers to break into the market (as discussed in chapter 2).

The court ordered Hollywood studios to sell their theaters. At first this seemed like a blow to the industry. The theaters had been used as collateral to secure loans, and they were a fixed element in the chain of movie production and consumption. But in the end the studios did more than adapt to the antitrust decision. The studios no longer needed to provide theaters with new films every week, and when they had a big film to release, they could distribute it more broadly than before, even to chains that had once belonged to competitors. Studios began to make fewer films each year and bring them to wider audiences. This new model eventually contributed to the rise of the blockbuster culture of the 1970s.

With fewer films coming from the studios, the theater owners began filling the holes in their schedule with more independent films, aiding the growth of an independent and foreign film renaissance and proving that the Supreme Court's antitrust ruling had achieved its goal of expanding the film marketplace.

Five years after the Paramount decision, the Supreme Court decided another landmark film case, *Burstyn v. Wilson* (1952), known as the "Miracle decision" because it involved censorship of Italian director Roberto Rossellini's short film *The Miracle* (1948). In the Miracle decision, the Supreme Court revisited the issue of film censorship, which it had upheld three decades earlier. This time the film industry graduated from being "a business pure and simple," as the court had defined it in the 1915 Mutual decision, to being a "a significant medium for the communication of ideas." Filmmakers finally enjoyed First Amendment protection, and film censorship ended in the United States, except on the grounds of obscenity. Filmmakers gained more latitude to address subjects that had previously been taboo.

These two major legal shifts—brought about by the Paramount decision and the Miracle decision—paved the way for a rise in independent and foreign film exhibition in the 1950s and 1960s. Films by a parade of international directors graced art house marquees: Ingmar Bergman, Luis Buñuel, Federico Fellini, Akira Kurosawa, Satyajit Ray, Agnes Varda, and more. Soft-core porn from Sweden and from American filmmaker Russ Meyer took advantage of filmmakers' new right to free expression. And American independent and avant-garde film movements found popular audiences.

At first, Hollywood ignored the rise in independent film, which conveniently kept audiences in the habit of going to the movie theater in between studio releases. Instead of competing directly with art house fare, the studios continued to make big-budget spectacles such as *Around the World in 80 Days* (1956), *Spartacus* (1960), and *Doctor Zhivago* (1963). The sale of films to television provided a boost to studio revenues, insulating Hollywood from the competition offered by the independents.

By the end of the 1960s, however, studio heads realized that they were losing a significant segment of the American film audience, profits were down. The film that finally convinced Hollywood that independent film had become more than a political and artistic niche was *Easy Rider* (1969). Made for a little over $500,000, the film grossed more than $60 million. A critical as well as a commercial success, the director-star, Dennis Hopper, won an award at the Cannes film festival, and actor Jack Nicholson, who had only been in low-budget films up until that point, was nominated for an Oscar.

Easy Rider is an encyclopedia of the 1960s counterculture. It follows two motorcycle riders as they travel the country experiencing America's clashing attitudes toward sex, drugs, and politics while rock and roll blares triumphantly on the soundtrack. With its episodic structure, use of unknown actors, explicit sex and drug use, and bold political statements, *Easy Rider* is everything the Hollywood studio system had been designed to avoid. Yet it was a hit.

Clearly out of step with audience demands, Hollywood took two drastic measures. First, the MPAA replaced the failing Production Code with a rating system, and, second, the studios reshuffled the production hierarchy that had reigned since the days of Thomas Ince, now making the director the star.

The Production Code was already showing cracks by the 1950s. Several studio films were released without Production Code Administration seals, and a new PCA regime headed by Geoffrey Sherlock loosened the organization's criteria. In 1961 Eric Johnston announced that the MPAA would consider a rating system, and in 1966 Lyndon Johnson aide Jack Valenti took over from Johnston with the aim of transitioning to a rating system.

In his first year, Valenti instituted a special "Suggested for Mature Audiences" category that was awarded to many studio-made films over the next two years. The first film given the SMA designation, *Who's Afraid of Virginia Woolf?* (1966), featured a slatternly Elizabeth Taylor and was peppered with words like "screw" and "hump." It was a huge financial success and swept the Oscars.

In November 1968 the new rating system took effect. Where the Production Code had been a one-size-fits-all model put in place so that every film could reach the widest possible global audience, the rating system divided films into categories. Each film now targeted a narrower public, but the range of films that could be made greatly increased, and Hollywood could compete with the art houses.

The art house films of the 1950s and 1960s, however, had more than just sex and profanity. They were made in a different mold than the star-studded genre films of the studios. What Bernardo

9. Elizabeth Taylor and Richard Burton exchange risqué dialogue in *Who's Afraid of Virginia Woolf*? (Warner Bros., 1966), the first film to receive the short-lived "Suggested for Mature Audiences" label. Two years later, the Motion Picture Association of America abandoned the Production Code for the rating system.

Bertolucci, John Cassavetes, and Akira Kurosawa have in common is that their films bear a strong mark of directorial authorship. In order to bring that authorial stamp to Hollywood films, the studios began either acquiring small production companies or starting their own director-focused subsidiaries. These subsidiaries had creative and financial autonomy, while the studios reserved the right to have the first chance to produce or refuse a new project.

Raybert (later BBS) Productions, for example, the company that made *Easy Rider*, struck a production deal with Columbia Pictures and went on to make Peter Bogdanovich's classic *The Last Picture Show* (1971) and a series of films starring Jack Nicholson. Similarly, Warner Bros. made a deal with Francis Ford Coppola's San Francisco–based production company American Zoetrope. Coppola proved to have a great eye for finding talented young filmmakers, and he launched the careers of writer-director George Lucas and screenwriter-producer Armyan Bernstein, among others. Less successfully, Paramount's entrance into the field, the aptly named Director's Company, gave larger budgets and lots of creative license to Coppola, Bogdanovich, and William Friedkin, only to see the three distinctive directors produce some of their least commercially successful films.

The term used to describe these directors is "auteur." The auteur theory had been developed by French critics to explain the personal imprint that Golden Age Hollywood directors like John Ford and Howard Hawks were able to place on their films despite their limited creative control in the studio system. By the late 1960s and 1970s, auteurism became shorthand for promoting the director to sell films rather than the genre or actors. And a generation of directors with marketable individual styles emerged, including Coppola, Steven Spielberg, Martin Scorsese, John Milius, Brian DePalma, and Terrence Malick.

They were all white men, and it would take another decade before a wave of women and African American directors began to claim the auteur mantle within Hollywood. During the 1960s and 1970s, however, many of the male auteurs had important women with whom they collaborated. Virtuoso editor Thelma Schoonmaker frequently worked (and continues to work) with Scorsese and other directors; production designer Polly Platt, who was married to Bogdanovich, worked on Bogdanovich's early films and later with producer James L. Brooks; Marcia Lucas, who was married to George Lucas, edited films with Lucas, Scorsese, and others; and editor Dede Allen collaborated with Arthur Penn, Warren Beatty, and others. All have Academy Award nominations, and all except Platt took home statuettes. One downside to the focus on auteur directors during this period is that there is even less attention paid to the many talented writers, set designers, editors, and others—frequently women—who put their own imprint on films.

This generation of directors is also known as the "film school generation," since many of them were trained at New York University, the University of Southern California, UCLA, and the

American Film Institute. And, indeed, as the studios became leaner, they outsourced much of the training of actors and directors to universities and to director-producer Roger Corman, who is a singular force in the industry. Since the 1950s, Corman (later in association with his wife, Julie Corman) has mined film schools for some of the most talented students, and a short list of his discoveries includes Scorsese, Coppola, Bogdanovich, Sandra Bullock, James Cameron, Jonathan Demme, Peter Fonda, Ron Howard, John Milius, Jack Nicholson, Nicolas Roeg, John Sayles, William Shatner, and Talia Shire. Corman's alumni often refer to themselves as graduates of "the school of Corman."

The studios also gradually moved away from having long-term contracts with actors, writers, and directors. Talent agencies like MCA, William Morris, and the Creative Artists Agency (CAA) filled the vacuum. They began to put together projects for their clients, which they could then bring to the studios ready to be made.

All of these elements created one of the most exciting and artistically diverse periods in Hollywood's history. And in an intense eleven or twelve years, the New Hollywood auteurs made an inordinate number of American classics, including *Bonnie and Clyde* (1967), *Midnight Cowboy* (1969), *Harold and Maude* (1971), *The Last Picture Show* (1971), *American Graffiti* (1973), *Badlands* (1973), *Chinatown* (1974), *Taxi Driver* (1976), *Days of Heaven* (1978), and *Apocalypse Now* (1979). Many of these films have entered university curricula and the home video canon, and they continue to have an impact on new filmmakers. By the middle of the 1970s, however, studios were beginning to funnel the creative energies of the New Hollywood auteurs into bigger commercial projects.

Big media

In addition to being restructured in the 1960s, all of the Hollywood studios were either sold to corporate conglomerates or became big media companies themselves. Many of the studios had essentially remained family businesses, with the original founders still at the helm. Larger corporations took advantage of Hollywood's momentary weakness in the 1960s to make takeover bids, integrating the studios with other companies and concentrating ownership across different media industries.

In 1966 the corporate conglomerate Gulf+Western decided to add a movie studio to its clothing, mining, and other assorted businesses. Gulf+Western took over Paramount from the aging Adolph Zukor, in his nineties, and Barney Balaban, in his eighties. The same year, Jack Warner, still head of Warner Bros., sold his studio to Canadian investors, who resold it two years later to Kinney National Services, which owned parking garages and cleaning companies. The new corporate era for Hollywood raised the risk-averse policies to a new level, and while New Hollywood auteurs made smaller personal films, the studios invented the blockbuster. These two cultures soon converged.

Before 1960, twenty movies had grossed more than $10 million domestically. By the end of the decade more than eighty films had crossed the $10 million mark. After that, a dozen or so films brought in the majority of Hollywood's annual profits. The studios moved to an oil-well mentality, in which a few blockbusters could make up for many mistakes. We tend to use the term blockbuster loosely to refer to an expensive production or a runaway success. But in the 1970s Hollywood created a recipe for blockbusters, which were designed not only to sell lots of movie tickets but to take the guesswork out of moviemaking.

Blockbusters, first and foremost, were "presold." They were based on existing works that already had built-in audiences. The 1978 blockbuster *Grease*, for example, adapted the long-running Broadway show of the same name, and it contained several well-known songs. The product had been tested, and the thousands of people who saw the play or wanted to were primed to like the film. In the 1970s, Hollywood developed blockbusters out of presold properties like *Airport* (1970), *The Godfather* (1972), *The Exorcist* (1973), and *Jaws* (1975).

There was nothing new about using presold properties. Edison adapted plays, novels, and the ultimate presold work, the Bible. But there were other ingredients in the 1970s blockbuster formula. Some were familiar. *Grease* was a genre film—a musical—and it featured popular stars John Travolta and Olivia Newton-John. But it was also a multimedia, crossover property. Travolta was a singer and television star who had just made a successful feature film, *Saturday Night Fever* (1977), and Olivia Newton-John was a pop star. They brought audiences from different media spheres, and the movie was destined to have a tie-in album, sequels, and a television spin-off. After a bestselling soundtrack and a weak sequel, the studio decided to shelve the television spin-off. Blockbusters had to be successful across media and offer profitable opportunities for more than one company in the media conglomerates' portfolios.

As a final ingredient of the recipe, blockbusters had to be "high concept" projects. When executive Barry Diller worked in programming at ABC, he liked to approve shows that could be sold in a single sentence. Steven Spielberg later said, "If a person can tell me the idea in 25 words or less, it's going to make a pretty good movie. I like ideas, especially movie ideas, that you can hold in your hand." High-concept projects have to have two elements. First, as Diller and Spielberg suggest, they must be able to be summarized (and marketed) in a phrase: "You can't be tried twice for the same murder" or "Snakes on a plane." It is even better if they can be captured in a single image: all of the promotional material for *Grease*, for example, used the image of the film's title twisted into the shape of a 1950s car.

The second element of a high-concept movie is that it is a combination of previously successful ideas: *Titanic* in the air might describe the 1975 film *The Hindenburg*, and "*Jaws* with claws" was used to sell a 1970s bear-attack film. Presold, high-concept blockbusters took no chances. They were easy to market, and rested on pretested material.

Under the leadership of producer Robert Evans, Paramount became extremely adept at producing blockbusters in the 1970s. With the backing of Gulf+Western, the studio bought Desilu, which had started by producing *I Love Lucy* in the 1950s and grew to become a leading television production company. And with the help of journalist-turned-producer Peter Bart, Evans bought the rights to some of the most popular plays and novels of the decade, including *The Odd Couple* (1968), *Rosemary's Baby* (1968), *Love Story* (1970), *The Godfather* (1972), and *Chinatown* (1974). These were not only presold properties that came with built in audiences; in many cases, like *Love Story* and *The Godfather*, Paramount bought the rights before the novels were released, and the studio insured that its presold bets were well marketed before they were adapted to film.

Under the leadership of super agent–turned–studio boss Lew Wasserman, MCA also mastered the blockbuster. Wasserman turned his talent agency into a fully integrated media company, with music, television, and film divisions. In fact, it became so big that the Department of Justice later broke it up on antitrust grounds.

MCA's film studio, Universal, may have cracked the blockbuster formula when it produced Steven Spielberg's *Jaws* in 1975. The talent agency International Creative Management (ICM), one of the agencies created out of the breakup of MCA, first packaged *Jaws*. ICM represented bestselling author Peter Benchley, who had written the novel and screenplay for *Jaws*, as well as up-and-coming director Steven Spielberg. ICM sold the movie rights to Universal before the book was published, so Universal could help market its presold property. And the studio created the perfect high-concept marketing campaign for the film. It was a shark-attack movie, a tried and true drive-in genre, only made with a big budget. The poster of a shark peering up at a woman swimming became ubiquitous, and Universal invested in a saturation television advertising campaign. The real innovation in *Jaws* marketing, however, was the decision to release it during the summer, which had traditionally been a time for independents, and to open it in four hundred theaters, "opening wide" in industry parlance, rather than rolling it out slowly. The opening of *Jaws* was an event, as so many subsequent summer blockbusters would be.

Very quickly the auteurs who made personal films in the 1960s and early 1970s became blockbuster directors. Lucas started the *Star Wars* franchise in 1977; Spielberg followed *Jaws* with *Close Encounters of the Third Kind* (1977), *Raiders of the Lost Ark* (1981), and *E.T. the Extra Terrestrial* (1982). These blockbusters reimagined the Hollywood genres that the auteurs had grown up with, and they provided the new multimedia corporate studios with franchises and "tent poles," ideas that could expand beyond film and into television, print, music, and video games. Hollywood mastered the blockbuster so thoroughly that many of these projects continue to exist, producing new sequels, prequels, reboots, reimaginings, games, and fan creations every year. In some cases, the blockbusters of the 1970s and 1980s have risen to the level of new American and even global myths.

Chapter 7
Home video and Indiewood

Just when the studios get comfortable, it seems, new technologies upset the status quo. Hollywood is always in a state of transition. In the 1970s and 1980s home video took Hollywood by surprise, and the industry spent the better part of a decade adjusting to the changes wrought by the new medium. But in the end, just like many previous technological revolutions, home video opened up new aesthetic possibilities for filmmakers, gave viewers more options, and increased Hollywood's profits. By 1986 video rentals surpassed theatrical box office returns, and by the end of the 1980s video rental stores in the United States outnumbered movie theaters four to one. Sony's early Betamax advertisement, "Watch whatever whenever," announced the new motto for the industry, although it would take Hollywood some time to adjust to the new reality.

Home video

Hollywood should not have been surprised by the VCR. Bringing moving images to the home and putting the power of recording in the hands of consumers was a long time coming. Edison (it always goes back to Edison) developed a projecting home Kinetoscope in the 1890s but only sold a handful. The French company Pathé began selling an amateur 9.5mm movie camera, the "baby," in 1922. In the 1940s and 1950s, engineers developed electronic videotape processes, one of which was funded by television crooner Bing Crosby's production company. Crosby hoped to develop videotape so that he wouldn't have to do two identical live television performances, one for the East Coast and one for the West Coast.

By the 1950s and 1960s commercial videotape machines were being used by most television companies, and video cameras began to show up on film sets in 1960 when comic actor-director Jerry Lewis started using a video camera next to his film camera in order to have an immediate look at actors' performances, a device which came to be called a "video assist." In the early 1970s, MCA/Universal collaborated with a consortium of technology companies to develop a laser disc playback system called Discovision, which eventually hit the market in 1978, a few years after the first VCRs.

Although Hollywood experimented with videotape and laser discs, Sony released the first consumer VCR, the Betamax, in 1975. Technology manufacturer JVC released a competing format, VHS (Video Home System), shortly thereafter. Betamax had a higher-quality image, but VHS won the format war. VHS tapes reached the goal of holding an entire feature film before the shorter Betamax tapes, and JVC licensed the VHS format widely to technology and content companies, while Sony exerted tight control over the proprietary Betamax format.

The proprietary-versus-open-format wars have been repeated many times, recently with Apple's (mostly) closed IOS mobile operating system and Google's (more) open Android operating system. Open systems have tended to win out over closed systems in the past, but, despite Karl Marx's adage, history does not always repeat itself. It remains to be seen which mobile platform will triumph, or if they can coexist.

VHS may have prevailed in the format war, but Sony, as the first manufacturer to release a home video machine, had the privilege of being sued by the Hollywood studios. More specifically, MCA's Lew Wasserman, who controlled Universal studios and MCA's large television production arm, filed a lawsuit against Sony. Wasserman asked every Hollywood studio to join the suit, but only Disney took him up on the offer. Disney not only had a large investment in television production, but the studio's executives worried about the impact VCRs might have on its unique business model. Disney owns a library of classic children's films and television shows, which the studio releases anew for each generation. If consumers started taping Disney shows and owning Disney movies, how would the company survive?

The case went to the Supreme Court, where the justices took the unusual step of hearing oral arguments twice. After the arguments, we now know from internal correspondence, the majority sided with the studios, favoring the argument that consumers could not tape television shows without the permission of the producers. But during deliberations, Justice Sandra Day O'Connor changed her mind and tipped the scales in favor of Sony. She saved the VCR's record button and fast-forward button (which allowed viewers to skip commercials) by a single vote.

This truly groundbreaking decision found "time shifting," recording a television show to watch it at another time, to be fair use (i.e., it did not infringe the rights of the copyright holder). Even making a temporary copy of an entire show, the decision stated, was protected by copyright law. All the evidence in the case suggested that people with VCRs watched more television. The court also listed examples of socially valuable uses of home video. VCR owners might record a presidential speech or simultaneous news programs for later viewing. Because VCRs had valuable legal uses, the court decided, Sony could not be held liable when users found illegal uses for the machines. The Sony Betamax decision changed the environment for home media innovation, and it made possible the creation of technologies from the iPhone to YouTube.

But Lew Wasserman did not give up easily. With support from MCA/Universal and other studios, the Motion Picture Association of America (MPAA) began lobbying Congress for an alternative solution to the problems VCRs created for Hollywood. The MPAA asked for movie and television producers to receive royalties from the sale of VCRs and blank tapes. Such a royalty would have acknowledged that unwanted copying took place, but at least the studios would benefit from it indirectly. Congress said no.

The MPAA also asked that the copyright first-sale doctrine not apply to videotapes. The first-sale doctrine permits consumers to rent, sell, or give away copies of media that they own. Used bookstores, for example, sell books without the permission of the publishers. The first-sale doctrine posed a problem for video sales, because once rental stores bought tapes from the studios, they were free to rent them repeatedly, collecting all of the rental fees. And the studios could not realize the full profits from films that found success in the video market. Congress again said no and refused to exempt videotapes from first-sale protections.

Hollywood responded first by trying to create what the industry calls a "sell through" market, cutting out the rental stores and selling tapes directly to consumers. Films with cult followings like the *Star Trek* franchise found fans who wanted to purchase movies to watch multiple times. And the occasional blockbuster, especially if it appealed to children, sold well when it was priced for families. Steven Spielberg's *E.T. the Extra Terrestrial* (1982) became one of the biggest sell-through success stories. With cassettes priced at $25, one in five US households owned a copy of *E.T.*

Most tapes, however, were priced at $65 or more, which discouraged personal ownership and required small video stores to be selective in the videos that they purchased. Even the biggest rental chain, Blockbuster Video, could not afford enough copies to satisfy the initial demand. In 1997, Sumner Redstone, CEO of Viacom, the media conglomerate that owned both Paramount and Blockbuster, brokered a deal for the studios to provide rental chains with licensed (as opposed to owned) copies. The stores would get as many copies as they needed, and the rental chain and movie distributor would share the profits from the rentals. Finally, Hollywood had found a system for profiting from successful video rentals.

To maximize sales from theatrical and home viewing, the studios further developed their system of "release windows." They first released films to movie theaters, then for television broadcast, and finally for home video rental. Studios have continued to experiment with these windows in subsequent decades, with some movies even being released "day and date" (i.e., simultaneously in theaters and on home video). Readjusting or giving up release windows has been one of the most difficult transitions for Hollywood studios in the digital marketplace.

Home video was more than just a new distribution outlet; it changed film production too. Films out of place in the theatrical blockbuster culture found success on home video. Music films, for example, did well on video, because viewers watched them more than once. *Flashdance* (1983), *Michael Jackson's Thriller* (1983), *Purple Rain* (1984), and *Footloose* (1984) were all part of a music-film cycle that took advantage of the video market. As consumers calculated whether to go to the theater or wait for the video, blockbusters got bigger, while more intimate films did well on video. In 1989 the blockbusters *Batman*, *Indiana Jones and the Last Crusade*, and *Lethal Weapon II* were the top-grossing theatrical releases. But the light caper film *A Fish Called Wanda* was the top rental that year.

It would be difficult to quantify all of the different ways that home video infused Hollywood with cash and creative outlets. Studios and independent producers began funding films through advance sales of domestic and international video rights, and in 1986 *Platoon* became the first Oscar-winning film funded with the presale of video rights.

Ironically, one of the companies that led the resistance to home video, Disney, may have benefited most. Disney released a few of its smaller films to home video early on, but it kept its classics like *Snow White* (1937), *Fantasia* (1940), and *Dumbo* (1941) locked in the studio's vaults. The 1983 theatrical rerelease of *Pinocchio* (1940) set off a clash at the top levels of Disney's management. Newly appointed CEO Michael Eisner wanted to release *Pinocchio* and other Disney films on video; the new head of the Disney's movie studio, Jeffrey Katzenberg, worried about the effect on future theatrical rereleases. Eisner won and twenty-one classic Disney films appeared in video stores. The profits rolled in and funded the next wave of Disney classics, including *The Little Mermaid* (1989), *Beauty and the Beast* (1991), *Aladdin* (1992), and *The Lion King* (1994). And these new films, in turn, helped Disney acquire the television networks ABC and ESPN and grow into a major international media company.

While Hollywood studios learned to thrive in the home video economy, the fantasy of the playback-only disc remained alive. MCA released Discovision shortly after the introduction of the VCR, and laserdiscs remained a high-quality niche market for cinephiles and collectors. But the digital video disc (aka digital versatile disc, or DVD) offered a new opportunity. The president of Warner Bros. home video, Warren Lieberfarb, saw the potential of the DVD early on, and he convinced the other studios to adopt the new format.

With DVDs, Hollywood attempted to avoid all of the pitfalls it had encountered when VHS tapes were introduced. Released in 1995, DVDs were at first available for playback only, although eventually recordable DVDs became widely available as well. DVDs carried high-quality video and could hold large amounts of compressed video, allowing studios to add extra features that enticed viewers to buy and rent them. New markets arose for unrated versions of films, director's cuts, and DVD extras about the making of feature films or additional scenes. DVDs also allowed multiple audio tracks for dubbing and commentary. DVDs were priced to be sold directly to consumers, encouraging the building of home libraries and consolidating distribution in the studios.

Finally, DVDs contained copy-protection software that prevents easy duplication. VHS tapes used a form of copy protection as well, but in 1998 it became illegal to bypass the copy protection on DVDs. Although ineffective as a tool for preventing piracy, copy protection allowed Hollywood studios greater control over which DVD players are compatible with studio movies on disc, and it allowed the studios to create versions of movies that can be played only in certain geographic regions, offering region-based price discrimination. DVDs could be sold at one price in the United States and at another in eastern Europe, for example.

DVDs enhanced viewers' relationship to movies and television series. Home libraries encouraged repeated viewing, and DVD extras enticed viewers to learn more about production histories and the events that inspired the movies or shows. Fans, scholars, and educators enjoyed access to high quality copies for research, teaching, and the creation of fan artwork.

Fan communities had existed since the early days of the studio system, but DVDs and digital editing software gave fans new tools for creating works that parodied, criticized, and further explored Hollywood media. With the introduction of internet video sharing platforms in the mid-2000s, fans found outlets for displaying and commenting on each others' work as well. DVDs may have seemed like an incremental change from VHS tapes, but the higher quality, cheaper prices, and digital formats allowed DVDs to change the culture of movie consumption.

Digital technology and the internet expanded the home video market even further. In the 1980s, most VHS tape players sat on top of televisions with 12:00 a.m. blinking on the device's clock. Consumers found VCRs complicated to set up and program. But digital video recorders (DVRs) incorporated hard drives and computer interfaces, creating sophisticated and more intuitive video recording devices. DVRs could be programmed to record favorite shows, entire seasons of show, or specific genres. They supported binge watching (viewing entire television seasons or series of movie sequels in a short period of time). DVRs became remotely programmable, so viewers could access their devices from a restaurant or while at work, and an add-on called a SlingBox allowed viewers to watch the content on their home video equipment from a laptop computer. The "whatever whenever" ideal that Sony had touted with its initial Betamax advertisements continued to triumph.

Indiewood

Hollywood has consistently been challenged by independent film movements, which have all been absorbed into the studio system, reinvigorating it. In the 1980s and 1990s, two very different independent film movements arose that pulled the studios in opposite directions. Both were helped by home video. Independent producers funded films with the advance sales of video rights, and home video provided another distribution outlet and source of revenue for smaller independent films.

The creation of what are called "mini-majors" led to the rise of an independent film movement in the 1980s. Mini-majors took advantage of Hollywood's blockbuster culture, undertaking expensive productions on borrowed money and hoping they would turn into box office successes. Ultimately, the mini-majors wanted to become new studios. Companies like Carolco, Vestron, Cannon, and the DeLaurentis Entertainment Group raised money by selling home video and global distribution rights; they promised unprecedented star salaries; and they invested in the emerging technology of computer-generated imagery (CGI). For a while, some mini-majors made consistently successful bets. But eventually they all took too many expensive risks during uncertain economic times.

Carolco, the most successful of the mini-majors, specialized in male-star-driven conservative action films, which were perfect for the era of HUAC star witness–turned-politician President Ronald Reagan. Carolco hit on the first successful franchise of the movement with the movie *First Blood* (1982), starring Sylvester Stallone as Vietnam War veteran John Rambo. The movie initiated a genre cycle bent on forging Vietnam War heroes. Carolco marketed the film by sponsoring a documentary on prisoners of war and deploying its public relations staff to help ripen the cultural moment for the film's reception. *First Blood* appeared to be so much in keeping with the zeitgeist that even Reagan praised it. The film took in $300 million in worldwide gross profits, and it spawned equally successful sequels.

Carolco invested in more action films, having another great run with a series of CGI-heavy science fiction films starring Arnold Schwarzenegger, including *Total Recall* (1990) and *The Terminator* series (1984–present).

In a short period of time, Carolco sought to move beyond making blockbusters and expand into a new major studio. Like Warner Bros. during the transition to sound or MCA in the 1960s, Carolco attempted to become vertically integrated. The company bought a video distribution chain, while also diversifying its production slate with some smaller genre films, including the history film *Mountains on the Moon* (1990), horror film *Jacob's Ladder* (1990), romantic comedy *L.A. Story* (1991), and thriller *Basic Instinct* (1992).

But Carolco ran out of money during a recession in the 1990s and bet the entire company on a single film: the flop *Cutthroat Island* (1995). The mini-majors turned the oil-well blockbuster system into a casino, and eventually they all lost. But before going under and selling their film libraries to the studios, the mini-majors permanently raised star salaries, and they successfully hastened

Hollywood's adoption of CGI, proving once again that most new innovations come from challenges to the major studios.

The mini-majors made the blockbuster culture of the New Hollywood even bigger. The other independent film movement of the late 1980s and 1990s extended the flip side of the New Hollywood era, the personal films that dwindled after the New Hollywood auteurs turned to blockbusters and franchises. What has come to be known as "indie" film grew directly out of the 1960s New Hollywood, extending the auteur-focused movement to incorporate more women and minorities who were (and remain) underrepresented in the studios system. Some of the directors that emerged from this period include Paul Thomas Anderson, Wes Anderson, Jane Campion, Sofia Coppola, Julie Dash, Tom DiCillo, David Fincher, Hal Hartley, Agnieszka Holland, Jim Jarmusch, Ang Lee, Spike Lee, Richard Linklater, Michael Moore, Alexander Payne, Robert Rodriguez, John Singleton, Kevin Smith, Todd Solondz, Steven Soderbergh, Quentin Tarantino, Robert Townsend, and Gus Van Sant.

Spike Lee (along with fellow New York–based filmmaker Jim Jarmusch) formed a bridge between the film school generation of the 1970s and the indie filmmakers of the 1990s. Trained at New York University's graduate film school, Lee made films about topics that would never have found a home in Hollywood. Like those of the social-problem filmmakers of the depression, Lee's early films centered on controversial topics: racism, female sexuality, and drug addiction. He funded his first feature film, *She's Gotta Have It* (1986), with a New York State arts grant and investments from family and friends. Shot for under $200,000, it earned over $7 million at the box office. Lee continued to struggle for creative autonomy, forming his own production company, 40 Acres and a Mule Filmworks, and supplementing his film work with commercials and music videos. Always at the forefront of new funding opportunities outside of the studio system, Lee went on to be one of the first major filmmakers to use the crowdfunding service Kickstarter to fund a film project.

Spike Lee's films were recognized by festivals and awards ceremonies early on. His NYU thesis project was the first student film to be featured at Lincoln Center's New Directors/New Films festival in New York, and *She's Gotta Have It* won a young filmmakers' award at the Cannes film festival. In 1989 Lee was nominated for an Academy Award for best original screenplay for *Do the Right Thing*. He didn't win, and the best picture Oscar that year went to *Driving Miss Daisy*, a film that could not have been further from Lee's provocative ensemble piece about the racial tensions ready to ignite on a street in Brooklyn.

But the generation that followed Spike Lee had a larger infrastructure of support. A range of institutions helped launch and sustain indie film, most prominently actor Robert Redford's multifaceted Sundance organization and brand. Based in Utah, what began as an independent film festival in the late 1970s grew into an educational institute, a funding entity, and eventually a

10. **John Turturro and Spike Lee, here in *Do the Right Thing* (40 Acres and a Mule/Universal, 1989), emerged as leaders of the independent film movement's alternative star system and auteur pantheon.**

lifestyle brand, selling clothing and furniture. Sundance really took off as a full-service film development center under direction of Geoffrey Gilmore in the 1990s, and the organization came to dominate the independent film world so thoroughly that by 1995 another festival, Slam Dance, was started to oppose Sundance's hegemony.

On the East Coast, the Independent Filmmaker Project grew out of the New York Film Festival in the late 1970s and created a screening venue, film market, and award ceremony for independent films. Dozens of magazines from *Film Threat* to *Filmmaker* to the online *IndieWire* began to cover independent films, and a cottage industry of books on how to make independent films sprang up.

Distributors began to focus on the emerging independent film movement. Law school student Robert Shaye proved to be one of the more successful entrants into the field when he started New Line Cinema in the late 1960s to distribute low-budget art house, exploitation, and public domain films. After successfully reviving the camp 1930s antidrug film *Reefer Madness* (1936) and new films by Baltimore-based exploitation auteur John Waters, New Line moved into production in the late 1970s. Throughout the 1980s and 1990s, New Line produced and distributed commercial franchises like *Nightmare on Elm Street* (1984–present) and the *Teenage Mutant Ninja Turtles* (1990–present) films, while its Fine Line division made edgy independent films like Gus Van Sant's *My Own Private Idaho* (1991), David O. Russell's *Spanking the Monkey* (1994), and Harmony Korine's *Gummo* (1997).

At the same time, brothers Bob and Harvey Weinstein produced and distributed a mind-boggling number of independent film hits through their company Miramax. One of their earliest coups was buying the rights to Steven Soderbergh's Cannes and Sundance winner *Sex, Lies, and Videotape* (1989). The film, about technology in the age of safe sex, was made for $1.1 million and grossed over $100 million.

The Weinsteins not only chose great material; they also created a popular audience for independent films through clever marketing. They sold theatrical documentary films without using the word documentary. Instead, they highlighted the films' political or real-world relevance and the auteurs who made them, especially Errol Morris and Michael Moore. Miramax, like Carolco, took unorthodox steps to create an environment in which films seemed timely and important. They managed to have actor Daniel Day-Lewis testify before Congress on behalf of the Americans with Disability Act during the promotional campaign for his film *My Left Foot* (1989), about a man with cerebral palsy who learns to paint.

Miramax marketed the film *The Crying Game* (1992) by convincing critics not to give away the film's surprise but of course revealing to readers that there was a not-to-be-missed surprise. The Weinsteins also realized the financial value of the Oscars. They put hundreds of thousands of dollars into campaigning for Oscars, and they were extremely successful at winning them. Oscars not only bring prestige; they also bring in more viewers for extended theatrical runs and for home video releases. Oscars translate into real dollar value.

By the mid-1990s, the independent film movement had developed into a mirror of the studio system, with its own auteurs, storytelling formulas, and marketing techniques. The independent film world had its own star system featuring Parker Posey, Eric Stoltz, John Turturro, Samuel L. Jackson, and Steve Buscemi. And a familiar narrative of low-budget triumph and Sundance discovery came to dominate marketing: film student Robert Rodriguez made the fast-paced action film *El Mariachi* (1992) for $7,000 while on break from film school; first-time filmmaker

Jonathan Caouette made *Tarnation* (2003), a personal film about coming out and life with his unstable mother for just over $200 on a borrowed laptop; and the handheld-camera horror film *The Blair Witch Project* (1999) was made for $25,000 and grossed over $200 million.

It is difficult to define indie film. Is it a genre, mode, series of institutions, group of people, or attitude? Was it really an independent movement when many actors, directors, and production companies seemed to move fluidly between Hollywood and the indie world? There may not be an all-encompassing definition, but by the mid-1990s all of the parts were in place for indie film to be a widely recognized movement.

Some filmmakers recognized the indie film scene as the heir to New Hollywood auteurs of the early 1970s. Directors Steven Soderbergh, Spike Jonze, David Fincher, and Alexander Payne paid homage to their predecessors by naming their short-lived production company after Paramount's failed auteur subsidiary of the 1970s, the Director's Company. The company name was more apt than its founders knew at the time, and the 1990s indie film movement had a fate similar to its predecessors.

Like BBS and the other New Hollywood studio subsidiaries of the 1960s, all of the 1990s indie film producers and distributors were absorbed by the Hollywood studios. In 1993 Disney acquired Miramax, and Turner Entertainment (which became part of Time Warner) bought New Line. In 2001, Universal bought the last distributor of the period to remain independent, Good Machine. The studios that did not snap up an indie distributor started their own art house divisions, including Sony Picture Classics (1991), Fox Searchlight (1994), and Paramount Classics (1998).

The lines between Hollywood and the indie world began to blur, creating what some have called Indiewood. The 1995 Oscars were hailed as the year of the independents, because so many films nominated for best picture came from indie producers. But by 1995, every one of those producers had become part of the Hollywood studio system, and the 1995 Oscar nominees signified not the year of the independents but the triumph of Indiewood: *The English Patient* (Miramax/Disney), *Breaking the Waves* (October/Universal), *Fargo* (Gramercy/Polygram), and *Shine* (Fine Line/Time Warner). As it had so many times before, Hollywood successfully absorbed its competition.

Chapter 8
Digital cinema and the internet

The mini-majors invested in computer-generated imagery (CGI) in the 1980s as part of their formula for making bigger blockbusters that could challenge the studios. The studios not only met the challenge; they made CGI a staple of Hollywood filmmaking. The incorporation of digital images into film and television is as much a revolution as sound, color, or widescreen cinema. And as competition from small and international media companies has increased, Hollywood has invested more and more in CGI blockbusters. Small independent companies may be able to create media tailored to the fragmented, niche internet audiences. But only Hollywood can put $200 million dollars on screen and reach the global mass audiences that have been the industry's purview since after World War I.

Computer generated images

CGI's genealogy begins with computer-drawn geometrical shapes, called vector graphics, used in 1950s military flight simulators. In the 1960s university computer science departments started to investigate the possibilities of computer graphics, and in 1962 MIT graduate student Ivan Sutherland wrote a program called Sketchpad, which allowed users to draw images directly on the cathode ray tubes of their monitors. Sutherland joined University of Utah professor David Evans to start the graphics firm E&A,

which helped to commercialize computer assisted design (CAD) software. CAD standardized the language of graphic design, and it allowed media animators to create wireframes, the digital skeletons that underlie CGI animation.

In 1965 Sutherland wrote an essay called "The Ultimate Display," in which he exclaimed that anything was now possible in the realm of computer representation. Filmmakers were no longer bound by the laws of physics and perception. Avant-garde animators John and James Whitney were already experimenting with psychedelic imagery, and their work influenced title designer Saul Bass, whose early computer animations for the credits of Alfred Hitchcock's *Vertigo* (1958) suggested psychological space. These experiments using nonnaturalistic imagery were the exceptions, however, and in general Sutherland's manifesto fell on deaf ears. Hollywood filmmakers worship at the altar of realism, and CGI has been used to create more realistic effects.

CGI began to take off in 1970s films, where it was used primarily to simulate futuristic computer displays. The science fiction drama *Westworld* (1973) used CGI to represent a robot gunslinger's point of view, and the sequel, *Futureworld* (1976), used wireframes to show a 3-D model of a hand displayed on a monitor. The latter sequence was created by Sutherland's student Edwin Catmull, whose team at the New York Institute of Technology would become (and remains) a leader in the development of CGI. In 1977 George Lucas hired Catmull to head the computer design division at Lucasfilm, which became the effects house Industrial Light and Magic (ILM). Lucas later spun off Catmull's division as the company Pixar, which was then sold to Apple founder Steve Jobs and later became the animation division of Disney.

The same year that Catmull came to Lucasfilm, Lucas used an extended vector graphic sequence in the *Star Wars* briefing scene that laid out the trench-run attack on the Death Star. (*Star Wars*' real special effects breakthrough, however, was not CGI but the use of computer-controlled models known as "motion control"). And in the late 1970s, the science fiction cycle set in motion by *Star Wars* contained many computer-display simulations similar to the trench run sequence. *Star Trek II: The Wrath of Kahn*'s (1982) "Genesis effect" sequence was one of the most elaborate. The scene in *Star Trek* is framed by a computer panel, almost like quotation marks telling the audience that they are only expected to understand the CGI effects as a computer simulation on a screen, not as an integrated part of the film's live-action world.

Catmull's ILM division took CGI to a new level in the 1980s, creating fully digital characters. ILM developed a computer called the Pixar Image Computer, which later gave its name to the animation division of ILM. The Pixar computer was slow at first; it took sixteen hours to scan one minute of film, but it could create sophisticated composites of digital and live-action material. George Lucas used the Pixar computer in *Star Wars: Return of the Jedi* (1983), and then it was used to create the first photorealistic composite CGI character, the Stained Glass Knight in *Young Sherlock Holmes* (1985).

After that, ILM developed a specialty in the digital morphing of characters—characters who could change shape. It became de rigueur for every fantasy and science fiction film in the late 1980s to have a morphing character. Some of the highlights included Joe Dante's *Innerspace* (1987), Ron Howard's *Willow* (1988), and Steven Spielberg's *Indiana Jones and the Last Crusade* (1989).

The digital-character breakthrough came with James Cameron's *Terminator 2: Judgment Day* (aka *T2*) (1991), produced by mini-major Carolco. Cameron had used an abstract CGI monster in *The Abyss* (1989), and Carolco had used some CGI the year before in *Total Recall* (1990). But *T2* contained a character, the T-1000 android, who morphs into and out of a liquid metal state throughout the entire film. The T-1000 was not depicted as a figure on a computer screen or given an amorphous shape, as in earlier films. *T2* seamlessly creates composite shots mixing CGI and live-action footage. There are only forty-seven CGI shots in the movie, but Cameron used them judiciously to give the impression of many more. In some scenes, the film cheats, very briefly using a stunt double in a silver suit to fake the appearance of the CGI-created liquid metal android. But you really need to be looking for the shots to see them.

After *T2*, even more CGI characters appeared, and there was speculation about doing away with living actors in favor of digital characters. George Lucas's three *Star Wars* prequels used an unprecedented number of composite shots as well as several fully digital charters, but Lucas saw the limitations. In a revealing sequence in the making-of documentary included on the DVD of *Star Wars Episode I: The Phantom Menace* (1999), Lucas is shown working closely with an animator to get Yoda's ears and vocal inflection just right for a single line of dialogue. When Lucas is finally happy with the shot, he says that digital actors will not replace live actors, because it is even more difficult to get a performance out of the digital actors. The animator adds that Yoda may be digital, but he is still created by humans. Digital characters actually add layers of human interaction rather than taking them away.

In addition, most digital characters are first played by real actors in motion-capture studios. Actor Andy Serkis has specialized in playing digital characters in *The Lord of the Rings* trilogy (2001–2003), *King Kong* (2005), and the "rebooted" *Planet of the Apes* franchise (2011–present), among other roles. In a motion-capture studio, actors wear suits that allow cameras to record the outline of their movements. Animators then flesh out the digital character by layering images over the outlines created by the motion capture software. Films like *Sky Captain and the World of Tomorrow* (2004), produced by Jon Avnet, and *Sin City* (2005), based on the graphic novel by Frank Miller, started to be filmed entirely on motion-capture stages, giving filmmakers free rein to superimpose the settings.

A small but interesting group of films broke with Hollywood's emphasis on creating realistic effects in science fiction and fantasy films to explore more painterly applications of CGI. *What Dreams May Come* (1998), starring Robin Williams, represented the afterlife as a series of living paintings, complete with wet paint squishing under characters' feet. *Pleasantville* (1998) switched back and forth between color and black and white, even in the same shot. And *Moulin Rouge* (2001) featured a long opening sequence that layered CGI and live action to give the effect of stepping into a diorama of late nineteenth-century Paris.

But these films, which seemed to take up Sutherland's call to let imagination rather than reality guide CGI, were the exception that proved the rule. Many more films used CGI to create realistic storms, animals, and crowds, from *Jurassic Park* (1993) and *Twister* (1996) to *Elizabeth* (1998) and *Gladiator* (2000). Audiences have learned to marvel at the spectacle of realism: dinosaurs brought to life or historical periods recreated.

CGI has become an aesthetic tool of choice in Hollywood, even when the spectacle is invisible to audiences. When Joel and Ethan Coen (the Coen brothers) wanted a washed-out, 1930s dustbowl look for their *O Brother, Where Art Thou* (2000), for example, cinematographer Roger Deakins did not use filters or special film processing. He shot the film in bright colors and used the tools of digital postproduction to adjust the color of the entire film (a standard practice today). It was also one of the first Hollywood films to use a digital intermediate process, going from film to digital to film again.

ILM remained at the forefront of digital effects, while its Pixar spinoff transformed animated films. After George Lucas sold Pixar to Steve Jobs in 1986, the digital animation team worked primarily as a military subcontractor. In their spare time, they created experimental shorts to be shown to other engineers at the SIGGRAPH computer animation conference. That year, Pixar hired animator John Lasseter, who began to insert more complex narratives into the Pixar shorts. *Luxo Jr.* (1986) combined new shadow-generating software with an elegant narrative, and it was nominated for an Academy Award. Pixar followed *Luxo Jr.* with a series of award-winning shorts. Steve Jobs, who at that point was no longer at Apple Computer, tried to sell Pixar several times, but he had already invested so much money in the company that it did not pay to sell.

Then in 1995 Pixar released the first full-length CGI feature, *Toy Story*. *Toy Story* did for digital animation what *Snow White and the Seven Dwarfs* (1937) had done for hand-drawn animation. It led the field with a technical and artistic masterpiece. Pixar had an initial public offering that made Steve Jobs a billionaire (amazingly, his first billion did not come from Apple). And Pixar followed *Toy Story* with dozens of successful animated films, including *A Bug's Life* (1998), *Finding Nemo* (2003), *The Incredibles* (2004), *Cars* (2006), *Ratatouille* (2007), and *Up* (2009).

As the technology grew more sophisticated, so did the animation. On 1995 computer hardware, the average frame of *Toy Story* took two hours to render. A decade later, on 2005 hardware, the average *Cars* frame contained so much detail that it took fifteen hours to render, despite a three-hundredfold overall increase in computer power. Dreamworks SKG's animation division (later Dreamworks Animation), headed by former Disney executive Jeffrey Katzenberg, and other studios began making digitally animated features. The technical and creative boom created a windfall for the studios. The average gross profit of the ten digitally animated films Hollywood produced between *Toy Story* and *Cars* was $200 million.

11. In the 1990s and 2000s, animators' ambitions continually outpaced technology. It took a computer more than two hours to render each frame of Pixar's first animated feature, *Toy Story* (Pixar, 1995) (*above*). A decade later, the average frame of the movie *Cars* (Pixar, 2005) was so complex that it took fifteen hours to render, despite a three-hundredfold percent increase in computer power.

CGI eventually displaced earlier forms of animation, and in 2006 Disney took over Pixar, making Steve Jobs Disney's largest shareholder and placing Lasseter and Catmull in top creative positions. As a result of the cross-fertilization created by the merger, Disney content was among the first released on Apple's iTunes video, and Apple created new media software to support Pixar. A new synergy between Northern and Southern California, between technology companies and Hollywood, was solidified.

From the internet back to the nickelodeon

The internet shook Hollywood's foundation. For close to ninety years, Hollywood thrived on the twentieth century's broadcast model of production and distribution. During most of Hollywood's history, a small, geographically concentrated group of people created media that was mass distributed and consumed by millions.

This was not the case during the pre-Hollywood nickelodeon period, in which exhibitors bought short films and curated them while mixing the images with music and dialogue. Nickelodeons were a hybrid of mass global and local media—they were "glocal"— as were most forms of entertainment in the preceding centuries: local theater, prerecorded music, and oral storytelling. In the nineteenth century (and before) a wealthy few could travel to a city and attend an opera, concert, or the theater. But the more common experience of culture was a traveling troupe, a local production, or a domestic recital.

Hollywood and twentieth-century media technology (sound film, television, and radio) changed all of that, and it became possible for a few artists to reach a global audience. Vaudeville performers were displaced by the Charlie Chaplin films that played on hundreds of screens at once. Movie-theater piano players had to find new jobs when synchronized sound put the New York Philharmonic in every small town theater. Much of the local flavor of entertainment disappeared.

Seen on a long historical scale, the twentieth-century broadcast model was an anomalous blip in the history of world culture. The internet not only ushered in a new epoch in entertainment; it also undid the broadcast model's one-to-many distribution system and returned the interactivity, local participation, and a many-to-many model of cultural exchange that existed before the birth of mass media.

Hollywood has reacted to this change, rather than leading it, but the studio system has also adapted to the age of media convergence and participation. The challenge of the internet is a big one, but the story of Hollywood's response should by this point be a familiar one of competition, adjustment, and triumph.

In 1992 media scholar Henry Jenkins wrote a book about television media fans called *Textual Poachers*. Other scholars read with fascination about this small subculture who did not passively consume television like proverbial couch potatoes. Fans, Jenkins explained, used television as a jumping-off point to write novels about the characters, to reveal patterns in television shows through re-edited videos, and to meet with other fans in communities of shared values. In 2008 Jenkins wrote another book, *Convergence Culture*, which described many tendencies similar to those explored in his earlier book, but this time he was writing about mainstream viewing practices, not a small subculture.

In the age of the internet, media consumers are active and participatory. They watch television while sharing opinions in chat rooms. They recut movies into music videos that comment on popular culture. They upload amateur fiction to the internet for others to read. They use video games as engines to create movies, called "machinima." The make parody movie trailers revealing film marketing conventions. They edit clips from television series to explore the lives of minor characters. A new media culture has emerged in which media consumers are also producers.

In 2005 a series of online video websites began to appear allowing users to upload and share videos, YouTube being the most popular. The immediate flood of videos uploaded to YouTube only revealed the pent-up desire for communities of remixers and active viewers who wanted to share their creations.

The Hollywood studios responded in a number of different ways, very gradually accepting the increased participation of media audiences. At first, some studios used copyright law to try to silence fans. One fan, for example, recut *Stars Wars Episode I: The Phantom Menace*, reducing the long political speeches and minimizing the screen time of Jar Jar Binks, the digital character who invoked offensive African American stereotypes. George Lucas had the video, known as *The Phantom Edit*, enjoined from circulation. NBC tested the waters of YouTube by quietly uploading a video, "Lazy Sunday," made for the television show *Saturday Night Live*, only to remove it after five million views and reupload it to the websites of NBC and the advertising-supported joint venture Hulu. An employee of the talent agency Creative Artists Agency (CAA) joined with experienced filmmakers to surreptitiously make a video blog, or "vlog," *Lonelygirl15* (2006–2008), showing that professional talent could raise the quality of new internet genres. On a larger scale, the media conglomerate Viacom, which had bid for and lost the company YouTube to Google, sued the video sharing site for mass copyright infringement; YouTube ultimately triumphed.

Over time, the Hollywood studios learned to work with YouTube and welcome user-made videos. In 2007 YouTube instituted the Content ID system, which both blocks pirated media and allows producers to profit from user-uploaded material. With the Content ID system, studios upload their video and audio libraries to YouTube. When a user posts a video, the system checks it against the studio libraries. Studios have the option of blocking the videos, which many did at first, occasionally leading to court disputes. But studios also have the option of allowing the videos to be published, with ad revenue shared between Google and the original producer, an increasingly common practice.

There is profit for studios in user-generated content, and in some cases popular YouTube content providers, or "YouTube stars," as they are known, can profit from their videos as well. In addition, many YouTube stars have had offers to work with larger media companies. A hybrid economy has emerged in which media conglomerates and their no-longer-passive audiences can jointly participate in the creative and financial ecosystem.

The surge in consumer-made media complements the studios' move toward bigger media franchises and tent-pole films with stories and characters that span media, a practice known as "transmedia storytelling." The narrative of the *Matrix* franchise

(1999–2003), for example, unfolded across movies, an animated series, video games, and internet forums. Producers of the popular science fiction series *Battlestar Galactica* (2004–2009) actively communicated with fan communities online to drive the narrative. And many media companies have experimented with the creation of mashup engines, software that allows consumers to remix commercial media, as a virtual equivalent of playing with action figures or acting out scenes from a favorite movie. In these experiments, media companies have exerted varying degrees of control over users. But even if the steps are small, they are moving toward a hybrid media culture in which consumers and conglomerates, amateurs and professionals cohabit the same media landscape.

While Hollywood studios began to create more internet content, writers realized that, like in the early days of television, their contracts did not extend to the new medium. In 2008 Hollywood writers went on strike, seeking to be compensated when their work was viewed online.

One unintended consequence of the writers' strike was the production of a self-funded three-part video opera created by highly successful writer-director Joss Whedon and his friends, family, and frequent collaborators. Their trilogy, *Dr. Horrible's Sing-Along Blog* (2008), is a fictionalized version of a popular internet fan genre: the vlog. It both celebrates and critiques the genre, with an ironic reference in its title to an early form of audience interaction, the sing-along movie with a bouncing ball over the onscreen lyrics. Just as fan works often explore the lives of minor or underappreciated characters, *Dr. Horrible* looks at the life of the misunderstood evil superhero villain.

The series' cult popularity made *Dr. Horrible* a profitable hit on Hulu, iTunes, and DVD. And its female lead, Felicia Day, was launched as an internet celebrity. At every level, *Dr. Horrible* highlighted the new models of genre, celebrity, and distribution that the internet enabled. Many new players began to enter the online media business, and a new cycle of independent production began to challenge Hollywood. After *Dr. Horrible*, for example, Felicia Day's own YouTube series about video gamers, *The Guild* (2007–2013), released a second season funded not by Day's small company or a traditional media company but by software giant Microsoft.

The studios' subsequent attempts to tighten control over online film and television distribution have generally backfired, creating even more media producers outside of the Hollywood system. The two largest subscription media streaming services, Netflix and Amazon, both moved into video production when Hollywood studios raised the licensing fees for streaming video. Unwilling to pay the new fees, Netflix and Amazon took aggressive and very different approaches to creating new video content, although both leveraged the so-called big data of the internet.

Netflix started streaming video online in 2007, and within a few years Netflix video streams accounted for over one-third of US internet traffic. When Hollywood studios began to price Netflix out of the market for licensing their movies and TV shows, Netflix

12. Microsoft took over producing Felicia Day's successful web series *The Guild* after it tapped into the commercial market for fan culture on YouTube, the Xbox, and other internet video platforms. In the music video "(Do You Wanna Date My) Avatar," *The Guild*'s cast performs dressed like their virtual world avatars.

used its massive amounts of user data to help guide it into the online video production business. Netflix had sponsored small independent films and documentaries, but its first large-scale foray into video production was 2013's *House of Cards*, a remake of the British series of the same name.

In some ways producing *House of Cards* was a safe and Old Hollywood decision. It was based on a presold property, directed by proven director David Fincher, and starred well-known actor Kevin Spacey. What made this move different is that Netflix's production team already knew every film and television show that customers had ever watched through the service. And they used the data to inform their production decisions. *House of Cards* was a critical and popular success, and Netflix followed it with a long line of hits, including new seasons of cancelled Fox comedy series *Arrested Development* (Netflix, 2013–present) and an original series, *Orange Is the New Black* (2014–present).

Amazon, also awash in user data, took a different approach. Amazon crowdsourced its new video projects, allowing users to vote for their favorite shows. It is easy to think that Netflix and Amazon are allowing the wise crowd of internet users to guide their media production, but both companies have used the data as only one of many pieces of information guiding creative decisions. If there is an algorithm for creating successful movies and television shows, it has not yet been discovered. Creative individuals still play the lead role in the production of online media.

As in previous periods of technological change and successful independent film movements, Hollywood has responded to the internet by incorporating its greatest competitors. In 2014 Walt Disney purchased YouTube's most popular channel, Maker Studios, for more than $500 million. On a smaller scale, Felicia Day's YouTube channel, Geek and Sundry, was bought by Warner Bros. subsidiary Legendary Pictures for an undisclosed sum. The

Philadelphia-based cable company Comcast has emerged as a vertically integrated powerhouse, acquiring film and television studios NBCUniversal. Comcast also has a major online streaming service, Xfinity, which has acquired licenses for much of the content that Netflix and Amazon can no longer afford.

As they have since the 1910s, technological and cultural changes have created new challenges for Hollywood. And some shakeup of the studio system is inevitable. But so far there is no evidence to suggest that Hollywood will not continue to grow bigger and stronger and continue to dominate global media production for the foreseeable future.

References

Chapter 1: Before Hollywood

"for the eye what the phonograph does for the ear": Thomas A. Edison, Patent Caveat 110, October 8, 1888, Edison National Historical Site Archives.

Chapter 2: The studio system

"Every foot of American film": quoted in Toby Miller, "Hollywood and the World," in *The Oxford Guide to Film Studies*, ed. John Hill and Pamela Church Gibson (Oxford: Oxford University Press, 1998), 373.

"The motion picture carries to every American": quoted in Mary Ann Doane, "The Economy of Desire: The Commodity Form in/of the Cinema," in *Movies and Mass Culture*, ed. John Belton (New Brunswick, NJ: Rutgers University Press, 1996), 121.

Chapter 3: Sound and the Production Code

"business pure and simple": *Mutual Film Corp. v. Industrial Commission of Ohio*, 236 U.S. 230 (1915).

"from which conclusions might be drawn": Jason Joy to James Wingate, February 5, 1931, Production Code Administration, Little Caesar File, Margaret Herrick Library, Academy of Motion Picture Arts and Sciences, Los Angeles.

Chapter 4: Hollywood at war

"are manifestations of fascism": *The Government Informational Manual for the Motion Picture Industry* (Washington, DC: Office of War Information, 1942).

Chapter 5: The blacklist and the Cold War

"Well, if you ask me literally, pretty much no" and "they didn't suit their purposes": *Hearings Regarding the Communist Infiltration of the Motion Picture Industry*, 80th Congress, 1st Session, October 20, 1947.

"The only thing red about [Lucy]": quoted in Thomas Doherty, *Cold War, Cool Medium: Television, McCarthyism, and American Culture* (New York: Columbia University Press, 2003), 53.

"dangerous and alien conspiracy": Elia Kazan, "A Statement," ad, *New York Times*, April 12, 1952, 7.

"No one can doubt in these chaotic times": *Lawson v. United States*, 176 F.2D 49 (D.C. Cir. 1949).

Chapter 6: The New Hollywood

"cinema has not yet been invented": André Bazin, "The Myth of Total Cinema," in *What Is Cinema?*, trans. and ed. Hugh Gray, vol. 1 (Berkeley: University of California Press, 1967), 23–27.

"If a person can tell me the idea in 25 words or less": quoted in Justin Wyatt, *High Concept: Movies and Marketing in Hollywood* (Austin: University of Texas Press, 1994), p. 13.

Further reading

Anderson, Christopher. *Hollywood TV: The Studio System in the Fifties*. Austin: University of Texas Press, 1994.

Bach, Steven. *Final Cut: Dreams and Disaster in the Making of Heaven's Gate*. New York: William Morrow, 1985.

Balio, Tino, ed. *The American Film Industry*. Madison: University of Wisconsin Press, 1985.

Basinger, Jeanine. *A Woman's View: How Hollywood Spoke to Women, 1930–1960*. New York: Random House, 2013.

Beauchamp, Cari. *Without Lying Down: Frances Marion and the Powerful Women of Early Hollywood*. Berkeley: University of California Press, 1998.

Belton, John. *Widescreen Cinema*. Cambridge, MA: Harvard University Press, 1992.

Biskind, Peter. *Easy Riders, Raging Bulls: How the Sex-Drugs-And-Rock 'n Roll Generation Saved Hollywood*. New York: Simon & Schuster, 1998.

Bowser, Eileen. *The Transformation of Cinema, 1907–1915*. Berkeley: University of California Press, 1990.

Decherney, Peter. *Hollywood's Copyright Wars: From Edison to the Internet*. New York: Columbia University Press, 2012.

Doherty, Thomas. *Hollywood and Hitler, 1933–1939*. New York: Columbia University Press, 2013.

Doherty, Thomas. *Pre-Code Hollywood: Sex, Immorality, and Insurrection in American Cinema, 1930–1934*. New York: Columbia University Press, 2013.

Elsaesser, Thomas. *The Persistence of Hollywood*. New York: Routledge, 2011.

Gabler, Neal. *An Empire of Their Own: How the Jews Invented Hollywood*. New York: Anchor, 1988.

Gomery, Douglas. *The Hollywood Studio System: A History*. London: British Film Institute, 2005.

Gomery, Douglas. *Shared Pleasures: A History of Movie Presentation in the United States*. Madison: University of Wisconsin Press, 1992.

Harmetz, Aljean. *The Making of Casablanca: Bogart, Bergman, and World War II*. New York: Hyperion, 2002.

Jenkins, Henry. *Convergence Culture: Where Old and New Media Collide*. New York: NYU Press, 2008.

Jewell, Richard B. *The Golden Age of Cinema: Hollywood, 1929–1945*. Malden, MA: Blackwell, 2007.

Lewis, Jon. *Hollywood v. Hard Core: How the Struggle over Censorship Created the Modern Film Industry*. New York: NYU Press, 2000.

Mask, Mia, ed. *Contemporary Black American Cinema: Race, Gender, and Sexuality at the Movies*. New York: Routledge, 2014.

McDougal, Dennis. *The Last Mogul: Lew Wasserman, MCA, and the Hidden History of Hollywood*. Cambridge, MA: Da Capo, 2001.

Muscio, Giuliana. *Hollywood's New Deal*. Philadelphia: Temple University Press, 1997.

Schatz, Thomas. *The Genius of the System: Hollywood Filmmaking in the Studio Era*. New York: Henry Holt, 1996.

Sklar, Robert. *Movie-Made America: A Cultural History of American Movies*. Rev ed. New York: Vintage, 2012.

Thompson, Kristin. *Exporting Entertainment: America in the World Film Market, 1907–1934*. London: British Film Institute, 1986.

Index

Index

Index